MUIRHEAD LIBRARY OF PHILOSOPHY

An admirable statement of the aims of the Library of Philosophy was provided by the first editor, the late Professor J. H. Muirhead, in his description of the original programme printed in Erdmann's *History of Philosophy* under the date 1890. This was slightly modified in subsequent volumes to take the form of the following statement:

'The Muirhead Library of Philosophy was designed as a contribution to the History of Modern Philosophy under the heads: first of different Schools of Thought—Sensationalist, Realist, Idealist, Intuitivist; secondly of different Subjects—Psychology, Ethics, Aesthetics, Political Philosophy, Theology. While much had been done in England in tracing the course of evolution in nature, history, economics, morals and religion, little had been done in tracing the development of thought on these subjects. Yet "the evolution of opinion is part of the whole evolution".

'By the co-operation of different writers in carrying out this plan it was hoped that a thoroughness and completeness of treatment, otherwise unattainable, might be secured. It was believed also that from writers mainly British and American fuller consideration of English Philosophy than it had hitherto received might be looked for. In the earlier series of books containing, among others, Bosanquet's *History of Aesthetic*, Pfleiderer's *Rational Theology since Kant*, Albee's *History of English Utilitarianism*, Bonar's *Philosophy and Political Economy*, Brett's *History of Psychology*, Ritchie's *Natural Rights*, these objects were to a large extent effected.

'In the meantime original work of a high order was being produced both in England and America by such writers as Bradley, Stout, Bertrand Russell, Baldwin, Urban, Montague, and others, and a new interest in foreign works, German, French and Italian, which had either become classical or were attracting public attention, had developed. The scope of the Library thus became extended into something more international, and it is entering on the fifth decade of its existence in the hope that it may contribute to that mutual understanding between countries which is so pressing a need of the present time.'

The need which Professor Muirhead stressed is no less pressing today, and few will deny that philosophy has much to do with enabling us to meet it, although no one, least of all Muirhead himself, would regard that as the sole, or even the main, object of philosophy. As Professor Muirhead continues to lend the distinction of his name to the Library of Philosophy it seemed not inappropriate to allow him to recall us to these aims in his own words. The emphasis on the history of thought also seemed to me very timely; and the number of important works promised for the Library in the near future augur well for the continued fulfilment, in this and other ways, of the expectations of the original editor.

H. D. LEWIS

MUIRHEAD LIBRARY OF PHILOSOPHY

General Editor: H. D. Lewis

Professor of History and Philosophy of Religion in the University of London

The Analysis of Mind. By BERTRAND RUSSELL. 8th Impression.

Analytic Psychology. By G. F. STOUT. 2 Vols. 5th Impression.

Coleridge as Philosopher. By J. H. MUIRHEAD. 2nd Impression.

Contemporary American Philosophy. Edited by G. P. ADAMS and W. P. MONTAGUE.

Contemporary British Philosophy. Edited by J. H. MUIRHEAD.

Contemporary Indian Philosophy. Edited by RADHAKRISHNAN and J. H. MUIRHEAD.

Contemporary British Philosophy. Third Series. Edited by H. D. LEWIS.

Development of Theology Since Kant. By O. PFLEIDERER.

Dialogues on Metaphysics. By NICHOLAS MALEBRANCHE. Translated by MORRIS GINSBERG.

Ethics. By NICOLAI HARTMANN. Translated by Stanton Coit. 3 Vols.

The Good Will: A Study in the Coherence Theory of Goodness. By H. J. PATON.

Hegel: A Re-Examination. By J. N. FINDLAY.

Hegel's Science of Logic. Translated by W. H. JOHNSTON and L. G. STRUTHERS. 2 Vols. 2nd Impression.

History of Æsthetic. By B. BOSANQUET. 4th Edition. 5th Impression.

History of English Utilitarianism. By E. ALBEE.

History of Psychology. By G. S. BRETT. Edited by R. S. PETERS. Abridged one-volume edition.

Human Knowledge. By BERTRAND RUSSELL. 3rd Impression.

A Hundred Years of British Philosophy. By RUDOLF METZ. Translated by J. W. HARVEY, T. E. JESSOP, HENRY STURT. 2nd Impression.

Ideas: A General Introduction to Pure Phenomenology. By EDMUND HUSSERL. Translated by W. R. BOYCE GIBSON. 2nd Impression.

Imagination. By E. J. FURLONG.

Indian Philosophy. By RADHAKRISHNAN. 2 Vols. Revised 2nd Edition.

The Intelligible World: Metaphysics and Value. By W. M. URBAN.

Introduction to Mathematical Philosophy. By BERTRAND RUSSELL. 2nd Edition. 8th Impression.

Kant's First Critique. By H. W. CASSIRER.

Kant's Metaphysic of Experience. By H. J. PATON. 2nd Impression.

Know Thyself. By BERNADINO VARISCO. Translated by GUGLIELMO SALVADORI.

Language and Reality. By WILBUR MARSHALL URBAN.

Matter and Memory. By HENRI BERGSON. Translated by N. M. PAUL and W. S. PALMER. 6th Impression.

The Muirhead Library of Philosophy

EDITED BY H. D. LEWIS

IMAGINATION

IMAGINATION

BY

E. J. FURLONG

Professor of Moral Philosophy
in the University of Dublin

LONDON: GEORGE ALLEN & UNWIN LTD
NEW YORK: THE MACMILLAN COMPANY

PRINTED IN GREAT BRITAIN
in 11 on 13 pt Baskerville type
BY WILLMER BROTHERS AND HARAM LTD
BIRKENHEAD

PREFACE

The present essay has its origin primarily in some of the remarks on imagination made by Professor Ryle in *The Concept of Mind*. Reflection on arguments used in that book led me to make the distinctions which I have indicated by the phrases 'in imagination', 'with imagination', and the term 'supposal'. I derived much help here from an essay by Mrs Annis Flew entitled 'Images, supposing and imagining' (*Philosophy*, July 1953).

I should make it clear that this book is mainly a philosophical study of the leading concepts I have mentioned: there is very little in it about the psychology of imagination. I should say also that although the questions discussed in the chapter entitled *Art and imagination* are, I think, fundamental subjects—What is a work of art? What is the role of imagination in art? I could not claim to have done more than set the stage for topics, which, fully treated, could occupy a substantial volume.

I hope that the tone and content of some of the discussion will not appear unduly controversial. Philosophy, it seems to me, is—much of it at least—a debate, a dialogue, something more akin to the proceedings in a house of parliament than to the advance of a natural science. And just as in a parliamentary debate a member will refer to a remark on the liberty of the citizen made by a member sitting opposite him rather than to a similar remark uttered by Edmund Burke two centuries before, so it seemed appropriate that this essay should contain some sparring with contemporaries who can, and possibly will, reply. I do also take some account of thinkers of the past, especially Hume; here I am much indebted to Professor H. H. Price's book on that philosopher.

In addition to my debts to books I gratefully acknowledge criticisms and suggestions given to me by Dr L. Bass, Mr W. V. Denard, Professor H. W. Johnstone Jr, Professor W. G. Maclagan, Mr J. K. Walton, Mr G. Weiler, by the Editor of the

Muirhead Library and by members of the Irish Philosophical Club, to whom a section of the book was read. I have also to thank the Editors of *Philosophy* and the *Philosophical Quarterly* for allowing me to reproduce portions of articles which were accepted by them for publication.

E. J. FURLONG

TRINITY COLLEGE
DUBLIN
November 1960

CONTENTS

CONTENTS

I

INTRODUCTION

A philosopher surveying the territory defined by the term 'imagination' finds it a dense and tangled piece of country. Its inhabitants are diverse: psychologists, art critics, writers on aesthetics, epistemologists, moralists, teachers and plain men. The topics that interest these people are varied too: dreams, inspiration, invention, education, sympathy, problems of knowledge, taste and other matters.

If we pass from general survey to detail and look at what the art critics and writers on aesthetics have said on imagination we may notice Kant's account of the 'free play' between imagination and understanding, an important element in his theory of aesthetic judgment. Then there is the well-known distinction made by Coleridge between the primary and secondary imagination. Coming nearer to the present, R. G. Collingwood tells us that the artist creates an imaginative experience in order to express emotion. Professor Susan Langer likewise affirms that 'the picture is the art symbol which expresses imaginative experience, i.e. the artist's envisagement of feeling'.[1] Professor W. B. Gallie, on the other hand, opposes such statements and urges us rather to study in detail, without idealist assumptions, the diverse workings of imagination. So likewise, other writers in the collection of papers, *Aesthetics and Language*.[2]

The views of epistemologists on imagination have been offered in various contexts. Plato gave it a lowly place in his scheme of knowledge. Descartes treats it as a bodily function whose operations are not guaranteed by the *cogito ergo sum*. For Berkeley, eager to show that God is the one true cause and

[1] S. Langer, *Feeling and Form*, London, Routledge, 1953, p. 386 f.
[2] Editor, W. Elton, Oxford, Blackwell, 1954.

yet wishing also to allow some efficacy to finite spirits, imagination witnesses to the activity of human beings: it 'doth denote the mind active'. For Hume's theory of knowledge imagination is central. Kant bridged the gap, possibly a gratuitous gap, between sensation and understanding by a liberal use of the transcendental synthesis of imagination. More recently Sartre has stressed the peculiarities of the imaginative consciousness. In opposition to Hume who had considered that imagination could fill the gaps in our sense-experience, Sartre regards imagination and sensation as poles apart. There is no question of the one complementing the other. Sensation is of the real; imagination is of the unreal, what is not-in-the-world. On the topic of the mental image also he is far from the tradition of Locke, Berkeley and much of British philosophy. For Sartre it is some object—a man, a place—that is imaginatively present to us; the mental image is an object, not of imagination but of a different activity, reflection.

Here Sartre is close to a view advanced by Professor Gilbert Ryle in *The Concept of Mind*. The latter writer indeed goes further and appears in this work to have no use for the mental image at all. Moreover, in this context as elsewhere, he opposes the intellectualist emphasis in epistemology. Imagining, he holds, includes not only picturing but mimicking, playing and other forms of behaviour. The child playing bears is using his imagination, yet he may not be visualizing at all. There is imagining-how as well as imagining-that.

Defenders of the mental image have not, however, been lacking. Professor H. H. Price and others have maintained that mental images do occur and that in some respects they are, *pace* Ryle, like pictures. Where are these images? They are, we are told, where they are. They define their own space. Possibly, indeed, as has been argued,[1] they are even spatially related to non-imaginary, physical objects.

---

[1] H. D. Lewis, 'Private and public space', *Proceedings of the Aristotelian Society*, Vol. LIII (1953); J. R. Smythies, 'On some properties and relations of images', *Philosophical Review*, July 1958.

From this rapid survey of imagination as handled by some of those who consider it a number of questions arise for discussion. Two broad questions are these:

(1) What is meant by 'imagination'?

(2) How are imaginative states and activities to be described?

We need not claim that this is the right way to set these questions. Indeed to ask them properly we may need first to know the answers. Roughly, the two questions correspond to the distinction sometimes made between analysis and phenomenology. In asking the first question we are enquiring what are the different things, whatever these things may be, to which the term 'imagination' applies, or has been applied. How does Coleridge's use, for instance, compare with that of Collingwood? Then, having studied the meanings of our term, we can go on to examine the different things, assuming they are different, to which it has been applied. We can scrutinize Hume's 'gap-filling' imagination and the intricate theory devised by Kant; we can try to decide between the opponents and champions of the mental image; we can ask what is the place of imagination in art.

A general objection to our proposal may be noted here. It may be said that the term 'imagination' is obviously used with such variety of meaning that it is a useless, or even dangerous term for philosophical discussion. I think this objection can be answered. First, it is, as we have seen, one of the philosopher's tasks to clarify the different meanings, and to study the special features each possesses. Secondly, we need not despair of showing a certain family connection, distant sometimes no doubt, between the different meanings. This connection, moreover, provides some justification for treating the different things we shall be studying between the covers of one book. If a book on 'thought' or 'mind' or 'sense-perception' can be accepted without serious misgiving, a study of imagination may claim to be a reasonable project.

17

B

Nor need we fear the charge that we are 'reviving an outworn faculty psychology', provided always that we remain sensitive to the manifold uses of 'imagination', and are cautious in noting whatever kinship they may have.

Let us begin then with the first of our two questions, that of analysis or meaning.

II

USES OF THE TERM 'IMAGINATION'

Past usage
A reference to the *Oxford English Dictionary* will show that
'imagination' has a variety of usage[1] and that it and some of its
cognate terms have had a chequered history. Take for example
the term 'imaginative'. We find (i) 'an imaginative child', i.e.
a child given to imagining, the (ii) 'imaginative part of the
mind', and (iii) 'an imaginative project', i.e. a project showing
inventive creative thinking. This third use of 'imaginative',
very common in art criticism today, is fairly recent. The earliest
instance given by *OED* is from Sir Walter Scott (1829). We
have here a word, previously used mainly in a descriptive
sense, which has now become a term of strong commendation.
It has largely filled the gap created by the discrediting of the
term 'beautiful'. No doubt we can trace here the influence of
Coleridge with his distinction between primary, or reproductive, imagination, which he equated with fancy, and secondary or creative imagination. The equation just mentioned
provides a new episode in the complex history of the relation
between the terms 'fancy' and 'imagination'. Milton wrote of
his 'Sweetest Shakespeare, fancy's child', and Hobbes, 'In fancy
consisteth the sublimity of a poet', Addison asserts that he uses
the terms 'imagination' and 'fancy' indifferently. In contrast
Ruskin tells us that 'The fancy sees the outside . . . The
imagination sees the heart'.

Fancy, it seems, has come down in the world. It was, how-

---

[1] I have used the word 'usage' here, though the chapter heading contains
the word 'uses'. I am aware that it is sometimes important to
distinguish between 'use' and 'usage', but I have not found it necessary
to do so in this essay, and I have chosen whichever term seemed to sound
better in a specific context.

ever, always the inferior term, as has been remarked by Mr G. G. Watson in a historical study.[1] Coleridge, he notes, wrongly thought that it was a new thing to distinguish imagination and fancy, but he did, nevertheless, provide a new distinction. Before him the criterion was a value one: imagination is reliable, fancy is not; imagination apprehends reality, fancy does not. For Coleridge both imagination and fancy apprehend reality, but whereas fancy merely assembles, accumulates, imagination builds a new edifice.

This distinction by Coleridge was, Mr Watson observes, novel, arresting and potentially useful, yet it proved too difficult to impress the minds of many poets and critics. The outcome was a great heightening in the prestige of imagination: it became a watchword for many. But serious critics tended to avoid both 'imagination' and 'fancy'.

As to the future, Mr Watson proposes that we should either get the Coleridge distinction clear and use it, or should employ both 'imagination' and 'fancy' in their primary sense, as described above.

Current usage

After this glance at the past, let us now look at current usage, and let us consider the term 'imagination', our main concern in this essay. To bring out its uses I shall employ an illustration I have used elsewhere[2] when discussing Professor Ryle's theory of imagination in his *Concept of Mind*. Let us consider a child, Peter, playing bears. There he is, down on all fours, growling and grimacing. We say his play 'shows imagination'. Let us see what exactly he is doing. Our description may be assisted by considering also what he might have been doing, but is not.

He might have been playing bears *in imagination*: he might, that is, have been lying in his cot staring at the ceiling and

---

[1] G. G. Watson, 'Contributions to a dictionary of critical terms: imagination and fancy', in *Essays in Criticism* III, 2 (1953).

[2] *Philosophical Quarterly*, Vol. VII (October 1957). The illustration is adapted from an example Professor Ryle himself uses.

playing bears 'in his head'. In fact, however, he is not in his cot: he is down on the hearth-rug making physical movements. He is not playing *in imagination*, not day-dreaming.

To take another possibility: 'Peter', his mother might have said, if it were bedtime, and he were sitting beside her ready for his evening story, 'imagine you are a bear: you are on an ice-berg . . .' Peter would have been asked to suppose, to consider what would happen if. In fact, however, he is not sitting quietly; he is not preparing to consider mentally: he is playing on the hearth-rug, the negation of bed-time composure.

There is another usage of 'suppose', a usage to which the sense just studied may approximate. If the lights were to fail and if Peter were alone in the room and the wind were howling outside, he might panic, imagining, i.e. believing, though falsely, that there really were bears around. As it is, however, the lights are on, his mother is there and Peter is in little danger of engaging in this kind of imagining. He is making believe, not believing.

To dream, likewise, is—as dreams are usually understood—to suppose in this sense. Peter wakes up terrified after a nightmare. 'Don't be frightened: it was only a dream. You only imagined the robbers were after you.' Peter, his mother allows, has had an experience like that of being chased by robbers, and he believed that the experience was real. But it was a false belief. So also for the hallucination. Lady Macbeth supposed, i.e. falsely believed, that she was seeing spots of blood on her hands.

At the beginning of the last paragraph I used the qualifying phrase 'as dreams are usually understood'. Dreams are usually understood to be experiences occurring during sleep in which the dreamer may do something like real seeing, real fearing, real believing. This usual understanding of dreams has, however, been recently challenged by what we may call the *story theory of dreams*. According to the story theory experiences do not in fact happen during sleep. A dreamer is a man who awakes under the impression—a false impression—that certain experiences have occurred. He is the victim of a series of pseudo-memories. The story theory, as we shall see in a later chapter, can be held in two forms—a factual and a logical. A man holding the factual form will deny that experiences do happen during sleep, but will not deny that they could. A man holding the logical form will deny that this could happen.

What we need to ask here is. Would the story theory if true require us to revise our conclusion that dreams are an instance of false supposal? The answer, I think, is, No. Peter, according to the story theory, will awake supposing, i.e. falsely believing, that he has been chased by robbers. As dreams are usually understood, however, it would also be considered that Peter falsely believed during his sleep, and this the story theory would deny.

The dreamer, I have just said, is a man who falsely supposes. But what, it might be asked, of the veridical dream? For example, you may dream of falling from a cliff, and awake to find yourself on the floor. It is a question, as I shall argue in a later chapter, how far this would deserve to be called a veridical dream. We can, however, take account of the veridical dream by a slight amendment: the dreamer is a man who supposes, usually falsely, that . . . Some dreams would therefore be examples of our first use of supposal; others, possibly the majority, would illustrate the second.

We have argued that a day-dream is a case of 'in imagination' whereas a night-dream is to be classed under imagination as supposal. It might be queried whether it can be right to put day-dreams into one class and night-dreams into another. I shall defend this classification in more detail later, but may remark here that we may say of a day-dream, He saw Buttermere in imagination; but of a night-dream, He imagined he was being chased by robbers. The hallucination, as we remarked already, here resembles the night-dream: Macbeth

22

imagined he saw a dagger; he did not see a dagger in imagination. The difference, I shall argue, can be traced mainly to the part played by belief in the day-dream on the one hand and in dreams and hallucinations on the other.

Peter is not, then, as he might have been, playing bears *in imagination,* nor is he supposing (first sense), nor mistakenly believing. In what sense, then, is he exercising his imagination? The answer, I think, is that he is playing bears *with imagination.* By this I mean, roughly, that his play shows originality, creativeness, possibly sympathy. He pretends that the chair is another bear, that the hearth-rug is a slab of ice . . His play is, in its own way, a minor work of art, a product of intelligence and sympathy. It is a work of imagination. No doubt indeed, like any other artist, he is drawing on his experience: he has seen and possibly studied the pranks of bears; but he is not merely reproducing, merely imitating: there is an original streak in his performance.

The question might be raised, Could there be a piece of play which was completely unimaginative, i.e. which failed to show imagination in any of the senses above? The issue here is partly factual, partly verbal. The factual question is, Could we have a piece of bear-like behaviour, for instance, which was completely stereotyped, completely lacking in originality? Well, could we? Possibly, yes; possibly, no. The verbal question is, Suppose we did in fact have such a piece of behaviour would we call it play or not? The answer is that we could call it either. Our choice might, however, be guided by some practical consideration. Thus, if we wished to arouse the concern of Peter's father for his health, we might say, as we watched his rather laboured movements, 'Peter's not *playing* this morning'. If, on the other hand, we wished to comment on Peter's low artistic quotient we might say, 'There you see a boy whose play shows absolutely no originality whatever'.

We see, then, from the illustration we have been studying that there are really three main usages of 'imagination': there is the usage which implies a process proceeding 'in the head', e.g. visualization; there is the usage as equivalent to *supposal* in the two related senses of that term, and there is the usage in the phrase *with imagination*. The usages are not, we may note, exclusive: Peter might e.g. play bears in imagination, with or without imagination; he might suppose with or without imagination.

One qualification concerning supposal, to which we shall later return, I shall state here. We saw that Peter, if he had been sitting quiescently, might have been asked by his mother to suppose that he is on an iceberg, to consider what would happen if. And we pointed out that Peter is in fact far from quiescent, so that it would seem he cannot be mentally considering, i.e. supposing. This is true, but not the whole truth. As we shall see, it is possible to reach the state of supposing not only by a mental, intellectual process, while immobile, but also by a physical route. It could be that Peter's playing bears was in fact a response to his mother's invitation, 'Suppose you are a bear on an iceberg . . .' or possibly to an invitation from himself 'What shall I do? I'll suppose I am a bear . . .' Supposal in our first sense can be reached therefore by acting as well as by quiescent thinking. And false supposal likewise.

Let us now enquire whether our three main uses have anything in common. I think they have in fact a common root, which is given by the notion of *imago,* a copy. The imaginary is a copy of the real: it is a short step from this to the not-real, the unreal.

The root is easy to trace for the usage 'in imagination'. Castles in the air, pipe-dreams, are imaginary, unreal. Take the next usage, supposition. Peter, let's suppose this is a deserted island. Peter constructs some suitable mock-beliefs, e.g. he pretends that this post is a palm tree, he entertains copy-expectations and copy-feelings.

Such supposition passes into false supposition when Peter

24

forgets that his expectations are copies: he takes the copy for the real.

But now, 'with imagination'? It is distinguished by its originality, its escape from reality, its freedom. To speak of copying here seems quite out of place. The fact must be admitted. And yet kinship can be traced. The notion of freedom gives the clue. In imagination we can climb Everest, or run a mile in three minutes. In reality these feats may be beyond us: we are tied down to the hard facts. So also to act 'with imagination' is to act with freedom, with spontaneity: it is to break away from the trammels of the orthodox, of the accepted; it is to be original, constructive.

The notion of the *imago,* the copy, allows us, therefore, to sort the various modern usages into a family tree:[1] imagining, of which day-dreaming is an example, on the one hand, and supposing, which includes *inter alia* night-dreaming and hallucination, on the other, are direct stems from the root. The term 'with imagination' corresponds to branches from either stem. What it shares with them is the notion of freedom.

A glance at the main conflicts and debates about imagination in post-medieval philosophy suggests that our three-fold distinction is on the right lines.

The debate between those who attack and those who defend mental imagery refers to the phrase 'in imagination'.

There is the Descartes-Sartre conflict: Descartes failing (at first) to find any clear intrinsic difference between dreams and waking life; Sartre claiming that the two are poles apart. The conflict here concerns the usage we have denoted by the term supposal.

When we examine the gap-filling, transcendental functions attributed to imagination by Hume and Kant we are again studying supposal or something akin to it, in one of its senses. A stone travels through the air, and we suppose, Hume asserts,

[1] L. Wittgenstein, *The Blue and Brown books,* p. 17.

that the window will break. So also, we construct, i.e. suppose, Kant tells us, a continuous time and space.

Our third usage, that indicated by the phrase 'with imagination', is concerned in Coleridge's distinction between primary and secondary imagination, and in the aesthetics of Kant, Croce, Collingwood and others.

If then we discuss imagination in terms of our threefold distinction we may hope that the major issues in the treatment of the subject by modern philosophers will be included.

Our three main topics are, to resume, (i) the imaginary, i.e. what takes place 'in the head', (ii) supposal, and (iii) the imaginative, i.e. what is marked by creative thought. Let us proceed to discuss these topics. We may begin with supposal which we shall find to be in a manner dependent on the other two usages.[1]

---

[1] In making the distinctions stated here I have been aided by the discussion of imagination by Annis Flew in her article 'Images, supposing and imagining', *Philosophy*, Vol. XXVIII (July 1953).

I should perhaps add a word here on pretending. Peter playing bears is, as I noted incidentally on p. 23, Peter pretending to be a bear. And what we found about play applies to pretence. Thus, pretending, like play, can be done in imagination or not. And pretendng can be done with imagination, and possibly not without it. Moreover pretence, like play, differs from supposal: Peter pretending to be a bear, does not suppose he is a bear; though, if he pretends hard and long he may end up by supposing, i.e. falsely believing.

III

SUPPOSAL

We have noted two senses of 'suppose', in both of which the word 'imagine' could be used instead. 'Peter, suppose (imagine) you are on the top of Everest . . .'; and 'Peter supposes (imagines) that he is really driving a space-machine'. In the second case 'suppose', as we have seen, equals 'falsely think' or 'falsely believe'. It is not so easy to find a synonym for 'suppose' in the former case. And here we must qualify our previous discussion. There are cases, similar to our Everest example, where 'imagine' could not be substituted for 'suppose'. Here are two.

(a) Let us suppose that we have a space of ten dimensions.

(b) Let us suppose that this point represents the church.

We could not easily replace 'suppose' by 'imagine' in these two examples. The reason is not far to seek. The suppositions concerned are not such that they could be pictured. We cannot picture a space of ten dimensions. Nor, though a church could be pictured, can we picture the relation we are asked to consider—that between a symbol and what it stands for. Peter-on-the-top-of-Everest is, however, something that can be pictured. We may conclude that if we are to be able to replace 'suppose' by 'imagine' the supposal concerned must be the supposal of something that can be pictured, auralized, or otherwise sensuously imagined. It must, to put the point tautologically, be imaginative supposal.

The conclusion we have just reached shows that one possible suggestion as a synonym for 'supposal' in the first of our two senses must be rejected. This suggestion is 'postulate'. 'Postulate' might work in 'Let us suppose a space of ten dimensions', where the premiss is formal and abstract. It feels too stiff in 'Let us suppose that this point represents the church'. And it would be plainly unbearable to say, 'Peter, let us postulate that you are on the top of Everest'.

I have no other suggestion to offer as a synonym for the first sense of supposal. One might possibly call it 'neutral supposal' to distinguish it from our second sense where the notion of falsehood is included. I propose however to refer to it simply as supposal plain, or plain supposal.

Plain supposal

I wish now to consider how this plain supposal is performed. 'Peter, suppose you are on an iceberg.' How can he comply? He might, as we noted in Chapter II, do so in either of two ways.

He might oblige by picturing the situation, or he might act as if he were in the situation. Picturing or acting: mental or physical activity. These are the two alternative ways in which Peter can do the required supposing. Perhaps this puts the matter too crudely, indeed, some might think, mistakenly. To suppose, they would insist, is not an activity but a disposition. Without granting all that is here demanded we may concede that when Peter acts his part—shivering on his iceberg, looking out for bears, he is inducing a complex state of mind, which includes expectations, preparednesses to act, and the rest. The term 'supposal' might be used of this end-state only, though I think this is a restricted use, and that we should more naturally include Peter's acting as part of the supposal, and not merely as a means to it. Similarly for his picturing. This might be thought of only as a means towards acquiring the desired disposition, or state of mind. But again we might reasonably regard the picturing as an element in, and not merely as a means to, the supposing.

Whichever position we adopt on the point just discussed we can say that when Peter is asked to suppose that he is on the iceberg he may comply either by an activity which is in his head, 'in imagination', or by an activity which is not.

Peter's activity can not only be done in imagination or not: it can also be done *with* imagination or not. His picturing may be inventive, novel, or not. So also his bodily behaviour; it may or may not show signs of talent.

Thus, to resume, Peter may obey the request to suppose by a response which is *in* imagination or not, and which is *with* imagination or not.

One other feature of this usage of 'supposal' may be noted before we leave it. When Peter supposes, in order to oblige his mother, his activity, whether in imagination or not, is directed: it aims at satisfying a request. But he might have engaged in the same activity without any such request. He might, as we know, have been engaged in reverie, or he might have been physically playing the required part without any external prompting.

In some cases at least, however, there was probably an internal stimulus: e.g. 'What shall I do now? I wish I had something to do. . . . I know—I'll play at being on an iceberg. . . .' Play where there is more than one child engaged usually begins thus; and where there is more than one child it often begins so too. Thus it is difficult to be sure that there is any undirected supposal.

False supposal

So much for plain supposal. Let us now consider our second usage of supposal where the notion of falsehood is included.

To imagine—to suppose—to believe falsely is a state, or activity, which can result either from mental or physical activity. Peter, playing soldiers *in imagination,* can come to suppose falsely that he is a soldier; so also if he plays physically, i.e. *not* in imagination. In both cases, too, the route may be followed with imagination, or not. And, in both cases, the activity which leads to the false supposal or false belief may, or may not, have been directed; or, perhaps, as we have seen, we should rather say that the direction varies according as it comes from without or within.

We are not, of course, suggesting that false belief is reached only as a result of supposal. False belief, which consists in having the wrong expectations, wrongly directed feelings, wrong preparednesses, may be produced or induced in many ways. Supposal is one of these ways.

Another way, as we saw in the previous chapter, is by going to sleep. In our dreams we are the victims, or the beneficiaries, of false belief. And this is true, whether according to the usual view we allow that dreams are experiences occurring while we are asleep, or, according to the 'story theory', we hold that the only dream-occurrences are false memories when we awake.

Still another method of creating false supposal is by inducing a hallucination. By taking a drug we can suppose that we are seeing objects which in fact we are not seeing, they not being there for us to see.

Are illusions also cases of false supposal? Yes, so far as they illude. If I am deceived by still water I can be under the illusion that I am seeing a bent stick, i.e. I can falsely suppose. If I then discover the water I may still see what looks like a bent stick. But I shall no longer falsely suppose. The illusion will have ceased to illude.

A similar remark would apply to the hallucination. If Macbeth could be persuaded that there was no dagger for him to see, he might continue to have a queer experience, but would no longer take it to be a dagger. The hallucination would have ceased to deceive; he would no longer falsely suppose. But the 'if' here is a bigger 'if' than in the case of the illusion. It is easy enough to discover the presence of the water which has created the illusion. It is not so easy for the distracted Macbeth to accept the assurances of his companions that there is really no dagger there. So also for the man who has induced a hallucination by taking a drug—alcohol or whatever it may be. It is this circumstance which constitutes the main difference between the illusion and the hallucination. But both, in so far as they deceive, provide instances of imagining in the sense of false supposal.

IV

IN IMAGINATION

So far we have distinguished three leading concepts, *in imagination, supposal* and *with imagination*. The concept supposal we have found to be parasitic on the other two concepts: that is to say, supposal in the two senses we have considered is an activity that can be performed, or a state reached in imagination (or not) and with imagination (or not).

What we are to do in this chapter is to consider the features of the concept 'in imagination'. Simply stated, 'in imagination' means the opposite of 'in reality'. It may well be that anything which can occur in reality can occur 'in imagination'. But, on the other hand, there are certain narrower contexts for which the term 'in imagination' is specially reserved. One such context is the day-dream: castles in Spain are castles in imagination. Day-dreams are stretches of imagining which have been distinguished by names because, presumably, they are stretches. We could, and do, have pieces of imagining which are not so distinguished. If I pause for a moment to see Buttermere in imagination I should hardly be said to have had a day-dream. We might think of 'in imagination' as a stream which sometimes expands into lakes. The lakes are the day-dreams. Sometimes the stream is a mere trickle: indeed frequently it has dried up completely. But there are also stretches where the current is strong. These stretches correspond to what we may call *directed imagining*. Day-dreams are largely spontaneous, involuntary: they occur without our asking. Directed imagining is a more deliberate affair. An orator, for example, may command his audience, 'Imagine what will happen next. There will be a flood of new taxation. You will be required to work longer hours. Food will be short;

there will be an end of hire-purchase.' The audience are being directed to picture a series of events.

The example of directed imagining just taken is a case in which the current of imagination is directed from without. But there is also much directed imagination in which the direction is from within. The historian, seeking to understand the events known (perhaps misleadingly) as the French Revolution may reconstruct in imagination a series of events in order to discern what pattern, if any, they display. Such imagining is not idle reverie: it is directed by the historian's purpose. So also the novelist and the man of science. A chemist may actually mix two substances on his bench, and see what happens. But he can also, as he sits in his study, imagine himself mixing the two substances and can imagine what might happen. Such directed imagining, we may observe here to avoid possible misunderstanding, can be done *with* imagination or not. Some historians and novelists show greater originality in their work than others. A man may imagine, but without imagination—just as he may play football or cook without imagination.

We can therefore use our term 'directed imagination' as a convenient blanket expression to include other-directed imagining—when we submit to the orator—and self-directed imagining—the imagining of the novelist, historian, chemist or other scientist.

The two terms we have considered, day-dreams and directed imagination, include therefore between them most or all of the stream we are referring to by the term 'in imagination'. Day-dreams refer to the lakes: directed imagination to the stretches with a well-marked current. There may, indeed, be short portions of the stream where the current is weak and which do not yet deserve to be called lakes. Here we have undirected imagining which is yet too transitory to deserve to be called a day-dream: the occasional image, the glance at some landscape that has pleased us, but which is now far from our view. Such imagining we can, however, treat as a limiting case of the day-dream: it need not be regarded as a distinct kind in addition to those we have already noted.

In the remainder of this chapter I consider the distinctive features of our two main kinds. I shall do this under the heading of what I shall call dimensions. Some of the remarks to be made here are trite and obvious and need not delay us long.

The dimensions I distinguish are receptive state, content, belief, feeling and controllability. Let us look at each of these in turn.

1. *Receptive state*
There is some variety here. The day-dreamer, for example, is usually relaxed. Directed imagination requires us to concentrate. Poets and novelists may produce the right degree and kind of concentration by artificial aids such as cocaine, alcohol or coffee.

2. *Content*
Speaking simply, the content is mental imagery, variously arranged and used. We shall be discussing imagery in a later chapter, so let us be content to speak simply here.

The content displays in varying degrees two qualities,

(a) *Originality*. There may be little, as in some day-dreams; or much, as in a symphony imagined by Beethoven, or a building imagined by Le Corbusier. Here we are on the ground of our other main concept, 'with imagination'.

(b) *Descriptiveness of reality*. The content may show little or none, as in some music, sculpture, and dancing, or considerable, as in some theories of historians, scientists and, perhaps, philosophers.

3. *Belief*
To speak generally, the absence of belief is what characterizes imagination, whereas its presence is a mark of sense-perception and memory. I see Jones over there, but I don't believe

33

C

he is there; I remember your repaying me that half-crown you owed me, but I don't believe you did. These are both odd statements, to say the least. Sense-perception and memory are, we think, means of discovering reality, what is to be believed in. But there is nothing odd about the statement, 'I can imagine what Venice is like, but it may not be like that at all'.

On the other hand there can be a passage, in the case of imagination, from absence of belief to belief. We can notice this occurring, in varying ways, both with undirected and directed imagining. The office worker, picturing the holiday he hopes to have, can pass from unbelief almost to belief. He can almost believe that he is now swimming lazily in the warm waters of the Adriatic. The author, imagining apprehensively the reviews his book will receive, may pass from fancy to something near conviction. Dickens began by not believing in Mr Pickwick, but may have ended with something very near belief—the belief that he was recording history, not fiction. The theorist, whether scientist or historian, may begin by half-believing his imaginatively-constructed hypothesis, and may end either by believing it to be true, if he is fortunate, or by disbelieving it, if he is unlucky.

4. *Feeling*

Feeling can operate in at least three ways in relation to imagination: as stimulus, as material and as companion. Feeling, actual or stored, may set the poet's fancy going. And then, as the spirit moves him, he seeks words to describe what he has felt and seen. If the words come, there may be an accompanying elation which in turn may spur him on. Failure will have as its companion impatience or disappointment.

The theorist likewise may be prompted to imaginative effort by feeling—the feeling of curiosity. His aim will not, however, be to describe what he has felt, but rather to discover the truth about the object of his curiosity. His imaginative efforts will be accompanied by feelings of joy, despair or satisfaction.

Reverie resembles here theory rather than art. It may have

its origin in feeling and be accompanied by feeling, but it does not aim at describing feeling.

5. *Controllability*

Philosophers and others have often remarked that imagination is much more subject to our will than is sense-perception.

We must under the present heading, distinguish all four of the previous dimensions we have noted. For example, as we shall see, the dimension of belief or feeling is subject to our will in ways that vary.

(a) *Receptive state.* By relaxing we can induce reverie; by bestirring ourselves we can end it. For directed imagination, as the name suggests, the reverse holds. Here will-power, discipline and such like, as writers know, are crucial. There are marvels of such discipline for us to admire—Trollope producing his daily quota of 3,000 words even when, a moderate sailor, he was storm-tost in the Bay of Biscay. Of course, good poetry or prose, satisfactory theory or cooking, demands much more than will-power. Few poets have written good poems with the bailiffs at the door. A dyspeptic cook will be unlikely to produce memorable menus.

(b) *Content.* This is less tractable. Over reverie we have some control: we can point our boat in a chosen direction, but we must then let it take its course. The novelist has some control over the content of his writing, though there may be a stage at which the story seems to write itself. He, no more than an accompanying reader, knows how the tale will end. The imaginative thinking of a historian is tied to reality, but this requirement leaves considerable freedom in the selection and discussion of hypotheses.

(c) *Belief.* As we noted already, the day-dreamer may pass from unbelief to belief. But this belief can be shuffled off by an effort of will. Similarly with directed imagination. The novelist's belief in his characters can be controlled. The historian or scientist may believe his theory, more or less, but if he is open-minded he will keep his belief *sub judice.*

(d) *Feeling.* We come lastly, in this connection, to the controllability of feeling. There is, in most imaginative activities, some control. We can arouse ourselves from a day-dream and thus end the accompanying feelings, though an emotional mood may remain. The artist and theorist can to some degree suppress or transform a feeling of impatience.

Several of the points we have noted in this discussion of control, provide possible comparisons with dreams. We concluded in an earlier chapter that whereas to see Buttermere in a day-dream is to see it in imagination, to see the lake in a dream is not to see it in imagination: it is rather to imagine, i.e. falsely suppose, we see it. Dreams do not therefore come under the heading of the present chapter. They do, however, provide some points of contrast with day-dreams which we may notice here—particularly with reference to our discussion of control. We have found that if we are day-dreaming or writing a novel or a piece of history then receptive state, content, belief and feeling are all, to a greater or less degree, subject to our control. There is much less control if we are dreaming. There are recipes for going to sleep, and thereby making a dream possible, but the best recipe is to avoid recipes. Sleep is better wooed by indifference than by courting. Some people can indeed end their sleep at will—an effort of will made before going to sleep; and over the content of our dreams we have a small degree of control: suitably unsuitable food or fiction are likely methods of producing nightmares. But there are no well-known rules to correlate the kind of unsuitable food we eat with the kind of nightmare we shall have. And ending a dream is not something we can do to order. As to belief, it is generally considered that here the dreamer has no control: in a dream, it is thought, we will accept anything, and Coleridge observed that there is no surprise in sleep. I am not sure that these universal propositions are certainly true. There may, possibly, be limits to the credulity even of a dreamer. But it is certainly understandable that his credulity should be immense.

He, unlike the day-dreamer, is totally, or almost totally, cut off from reality—reality as revealed by his senses. Only logic, perhaps, can limit what he will imagine. And it is a question what limit logic sets. Can we, for example, accept in a dream something contrary to the law of excluded middle? If we can, what about the law of non-contradiction?

With emotion as with belief, the dreamer's control is slight. He cannot bring himself to look away from the monstrous lorry that is bearing down upon him, or the abyss that yawns below him. His terror cannot be diminished by evasive action.

Here, as in other respects, dreams have much in common with hallucinations—certainly the hallucinations of the mentally diseased. There is, with such hallucinations, as with the dream, little or no control as to onset, credulity and emotion.

These points of comparison between the dream and between phenomena of waking life we shall take up again when we discuss dreams at greater length in the next two chapters.

V

DREAMS—WHAT THEY ARE

'I never dreamt of such a thing; I never imagined such a thing.' Or 'Don't be frightened, child; it was only a dream, you only imagined it'. Common speech suggests a link between dreams and imagination. It suggests that when we are dreaming, we are imagining, in some sense. I have in earlier chapters advanced the view that the sense here is that of supposal, and usually false supposal: the dreamer is supposing that he sees this, hears that or feels something else. But I did not argue for this view at any length. I shall now try to show why I think it to be correct. But before I attempt this positive task I must spend some time in considering a rival view. This view, mentioned briefly in chapter II, I have called the *story theory of dreams*. Roughly, it is this. Common speech may suggest, as we have just seen, that dreams are experiences which occur when we are asleep. But, according to the story theory, common speech is here mistaken: there are, indeed perhaps can be, no experiences when we are asleep. All that happens is that we awake ready to tell certain stories—that we were being chased by robbers, were falling over a cliff, or whatever it may be.

The story theory can of course be developed and refined. And I shall be considering in some detail a recent skilfully defended statement of it. Here we may note that the view can be, and has been, advanced in two different forms. There is the view that there are in fact no sleeping experiences; and there are no sleeping experiences, according to this view, for the good reason that there can be none: it is absurd, senseless to talk of a sleeping experience.

This variety of the view I shall call the logical form of the story theory.

But, secondly, it has been maintained that as a matter of fact—not as a matter of logic—sleeping experiences do not occur. They could occur, but they do not. This version of the view I shall call the factual form of the story theory.

The main difference, then, between the two forms, so far as dreams are concerned, is this: according to the factual form, dreams, i.e. experiences of a certain kind, could occur during sleep, but they do not; whereas, according to the logical form, dreams could not occur during sleep.

As with more than one current controversy among philosophers, the man who set the ball rolling—the villain of the piece, according to some—is Descartes. In the first of his *Meditations* he poses a problem about dreams, confesses his failure to answer this problem, and uses this failure to assist his process of 'methodical doubt'.

We shall be considering Descartes' problem in some detail in the next chapter. Here we may note that Descartes does assume, with common speech, that experiences do occur while we are asleep—experiences which resemble seeing, doubting and believing. A recent contribution to the debate over this assumption, a debate begun by the late Miss Margaret Macdonald with her provocative paper 'Sleeping and waking',[1] is Professor Norman Malcolm's book *Dreaming*,[2] which sets out the story theory in its logical form in detail and defends it with ingenuity and resource. It will be his statement that I shall have mainly in view in the following discussion.

The debate just referred to has turned chiefly on the logical form of the story theory. It is not easy to find a detailed statement and scrutiny of the story theory in its factual form; but it achieved a mention in a fairly recent symposium,[3] and Professor Malcolm gives it a passing reference in his book. It is, we may guess, the kind of theory that might appeal to an

[1] M. Macdonald, *Mind*, April 1953.
[2] N. Malcolm, *Dreaming*, London, Routledge, 1959, in *Studies in Philosophical Psychology*, ed. R. F. Holland.
[3] A. R. Manser, pp. 226 f. in the *Proceedings of the Aristotelian Society*, Supplementary Volume XXX. Mr Manser does not defend the theory.

economically-minded natural scientist, with stern standards of proof.

Let us now proceed to detailed examination of the story theory. I shall begin with the logical form which, as I have remarked, has received the most extensive treatment.

Statement of the story theory (logical form)

Here, as already stated, I shall have chiefly in view the theory as put forward by Malcolm. The theory, as advanced by him, has a negative and a positive side to it. Negatively, he denies that experiences can occur while we are asleep. Positively he supplies a theory of dreams which is intended to complement this denial. Let us look at these negative and positive theses in turn.

I can only give here the barest sketch of his argument which in any case will probably be familiar to my readers. Having argued that neither the assertion nor the judgment 'I am asleep' can be sensibly made, Malcolm claims that in like manner it can be proved that 'it is nonsensical to suppose that while a person is asleep he could make any judgment' (p. 36).[1] His method of proving this is typical of his argument throughout. Suppose the alleged dream-judgment were that the law of excluded middle is false. I cannot verify that as you lie asleep you are making that judgment. Nor can you verify it: you cannot have been aware of being asleep when you made the judgment.

Nor can you infer you were asleep: how would you try to make such an inference? You could not do so by arguing that you had not made the judgment before you went to sleep, nor made it after you awoke, so that you must have made it while asleep: this argument would be inconclusive, because the facts can be explained by just supposing that you remember making the judgment, without your having actually made it. Compare the man who claims to solve a problem while asleep. He had not the solution when he went to sleep: he has it when

---

[1] The references are to Professor Malcolm's book, cited above.

he awakes. But that could be the whole story. And it must be the whole story because to assert that he got the solution while asleep is to assert what cannot be verified.

You might claim that the judgment occurred during a dream, and therefore during sleep. Here we must anticipate Malcolm's positive theory of dreaming. The fact that the judgment forms part of a dream does not, he will be asserting, imply that the judgment occurred during sleep: and he will be making this assertion because he will be denying, or finding no sense in, the statement that dreams occur during sleep.

Nor will it help to claim that the judgment occurred, not as part of, but along with a dream, just as people sometimes assert that they realized they were dreaming—the realization not forming part of the dream. The most that such a claim if valid, would do is to place the alleged judgment in the same time as the events of the dream, and that time is not physical time.

The electro-encephalograph will not help either. Suppose it has been found that, you being awake, your brain registers B whenever you make a judgment J. It does not follow that if you are asleep and your brain registers B you will be making the judgment J. Such a conclusion is 'logically incapable of confirmation. It would be impossible to know whether this conclusion was true or false' (p. 43).

Malcolm concludes that 'since we do not know what the facts would have to be in order for it to be true that someone made a judgment while asleep, it is a foregone conclusion that any attempt to "infer" that unintelligible state of affairs if only with probability will get nowhere' (p. 44).

The remainder of Malcolm's negative thesis is easy going. The line of argument already used 'can be made into a proof that thinking during sleep, reasoning in sleep, imagining in sleep and so on, are all unintelligible notions. The things just mentioned are all examples of mental *activities,* but this is not essential to the proof. It works just as well for "passivities" like fear, anxiety, joy; illusions and hallucinations; and

41

imagery' (p. 45). Take imagery. I cannot verify that you, as you lie asleep before me, are having mental imagery; and your testimony is worthless: what you testify to cannot be verified; and physiology is again of no help.

But if no experiences of any kind can occur while we are asleep, what are we to say of dreams? In common speech we use such expressions as 'I went to sleep and dreamt', or 'She passed the night in a dreamless sleep'. Common speech therefore proceeds on the assumption that we can and do have experiences while asleep. This assumption, however, is what Malcolm has just denied. If he is right, then common speech cannot be trusted here. If to dream is to have an experience, then dreams cannot occur during sleep.

What view then does Malcolm offer of dreams? What is his positive thesis concerning them? We can begin by taking an example. Suppose I awake and declare, like the poet, 'I dreamt that I dwelt in marble halls'. According to Malcolm what I have stated is that I was under the impression that I dwelt in marble halls; but since the marble walls cannot be found, it must be a dream. One or two quotations from Malcolm's book will clarify this statement of his theory.

'Aristotle says that a dream is a kind of illusory sense-presentation occurring in sleep . . . Descartes thought that in dreaming we reason and judge in exactly the same sense that we do when awake. Hobbes believed that dreams are "the imaginations of them that sleep". Other philosophers think that dreaming is having images or even hallucinations in sleep.

'These opinions can be seen to be mistaken. The argument of Chapters 9 and 10 shows, I think, that the idea that someone might reason, judge, imagine, or have impressions, presentations, illusions or hallucinations, while asleep, is a meaningless idea in the sense that we have no conception of what could establish that these things did or did not occur. We know perfectly well, however, what establishes that a person dreamt while he slept—namely, his telling a dream. This clear difference in possibility of verification shows that dreams are none of the things that philosophers have commonly supposed them to be.'

Admittedly, Malcolm is referring here to the *criterion* for having dreamt, but on p. 55 he writes 'What we must say, although it seems paradoxical, is that the concept of dreaming is derived, not from dreaming, but from descriptions of dreams, i.e. from the familiar phenomenon that we call "telling a dream". If after waking from sleep a child tells us that he saw and did and thought various things, none of which could be true, and if his relation of these incidents has spontaneity and no appearance of invention, then we may say to him "it was a dream". We do not question whether he really had a dream or if it merely seems to him that he did.'

And on p. 59 he states, 'Indeed I am not trying to say what dreaming *is*: I do not understand what it would mean to do that. I merely set forth the reminder that in our daily discourse about dreams what we take as determining beyond question that a man dreamt is that in sincerity he should tell a dream or say he had one.' Finally, on p. 65, 'I am inclined to believe that statements of the form "I dreamt so and so" are always inferential in nature. I do not mean that one always arrives at them by explicit processes of inference but rather that one might always defend them as conclusions from certain facts or supposed facts. If someone were to ask you how you knew that you dreamt so and so, you could always mention something that you supposed proved or made probable that the thing in question did not occur and that therefore you dreamt it.

'What can have no justification and requires none is your statement that you have the *impression* that so and so occurred. (You may or may not believe that it did occur.) In this sense you cannot find out that you dreamt, although you can find out that someone else dreamt. What it does make sense to find out is whether your impression corresponds with reality, and to discover that it does not is to discover that you had a dream.'

Certain objections to Malcolm's theory will probably come to mind at once. I shall mention here a few of those he considers himself. There is the continuity objection. We awake feeling terrified after, so we think, the terror of a bad dream. The one terror appears to be continuous with the other. If the waking terror occurs, does it not follow that the dreaming terror was an event which occurred also—when we were asleep?

Then there is what I shall call the asthmatic objection, taken from an article by R. M. Yost, Jr and D. Kalish.[1] An asthmatic sufferer dreams that he is suffocating. Now he is in fact suffocating because of his asthma. Does his dream-feeling not therefore occur? The feeling may differ in some respects from a waking feeling, but it is still a mental happening while asleep, the kind of thing Malcolm has denied.

Again, there is the objection that dreams do seem to have a location in time. They may occur just before we awake, or, at the least, some time during the night.

Lastly, physiology supplies an objection of a kind we have noticed already in another context. Suppose that in waking life a specific secretion of adrenalin is associated with fear; then if in sleep the same secretion occurs, have we not some presumption here in favour of sleeping fear—especially if the dreamer awakes claiming to have feared?

Since Malcolm holds that it is senseless to speak of having any kind of experience while asleep, and since all these objections aim at proving that we do have experiences while asleep, he must consider that the objections are bound to be fallacious. It is useful, however, to notice how he deals with the facts on which the objections are based.

The continuity objection he replies to by remarking that since we awoke with a terrifying impression (his theory of

---

[1] *Philosophical Quarterly*, April 1955, p. 120. Professor Malcolm's theory as stated in an article, *Philosophical Review* (1956), has been carefully examined in two papers by Yost, *Philosophical Quarterly*, April and July, 1959.

what it is to have had a terrifying dream) there is no wonder that we are, in fact, terrified (p. 92).

The asthmatic objection he deals with by maintaining that if the sufferer was in fact suffocating, as was postulated, then he was not fully asleep. Now to have dreamt he must have been fully asleep; otherwise he might have been only day-dreaming (p. 99).

Then there is the claim that we can locate dreams in time—the time during which we were asleep. To this Malcolm replies that such a claim is too vague: no scientist would accept it as locating dreams in physical, public time (p. 76).

The physiological objection is ruled out on the ground that the analogy will not work: we are trying to extrapolate from experience to non-experience and this is illegitimate (p. 75).

Now, whether or not we like Malcolm's replies to these various objections, it is clear that some such replies must be given—provided always that experiences cannot, as he has maintained, occur during sleep. But, of course, if Malcolm were mistaken on this fundamental point, then the objections would require to be reconsidered and would not be ruled out from the start. They would then, it will be seen—this is a point to which we shall return—become objections to the story theory in its *factual* form.

Discussion of the story theory (logical form)

Let us now, therefore, consider whether Malcolm has really established the fundamental point in his position, namely, that it is senseless to talk of experiences occurring while we are asleep: and that it is senseless because the occurrence of such experiences could not be verified by those observing the sleeper, nor could they be verified by the sleeper himself.

Let us take a concrete case. Suppose we are looking at a sleeping child, a lad of ten or so. As we look, a smile passes over his face, or he calls out in a tone of alarm, Go away, go away. We say, Ah, he must be having a dream: a pleasant dream, or a frightening dream, as the case may be. Just then the child awakes, gradually becomes aware of us, and says, I was just having a lovely dream. And he proceeds to tell us of it: he was on a wonderful island; he was swimming in a coral pool . . . Now we may well think he is referring to experiences he had some time within the last few minutes. But, according to Malcolm, there were no such experiences; indeed, there could have been no such experiences. All it makes sense to say is that the child has awakened under the impression that he was on his island, and that it was a false impression.

What Malcolm wants us to believe, therefore, is that when we look at the sleeping child and say, He must be having a pleasant dream, we are talking nonsense. Now this, it seems to me, is very hard to accept. Is there any good reason why we should accept it? The reason Malcolm gives is that no possible observation can verify the statement that the child is having an experience while asleep. We lookers-on cannot verify it, neither can the child himself.

But now, is it quite true that the child cannot verify it? The answer to this question depends on what means of verification we allow. The child awakes under the impression, say, that a bad robber was running after him down a lonely road. He is sure that something frightening happened. 'It's all right,' we tell him, 'there wasn't any bad robber, you weren't out on the road. You only imagined it.'

Now we do not deny that something, in fact, happened. We accept the child's evidence up to a point, just as, though up to a different point, we might accept his evidence, given in broad daylight, that he has just seen a policeman in the garden, or just had a pleasant day-dream. Unless we have reason to distrust his memory, or his capacity to tell the truth, we accept his stories of what happens to him in waking life. Why should we refuse to accept his conviction that something frightening happened to him while asleep? And if we distrust his conviction here why should we not distrust his memory-convictions elsewhere? In so far as the child's memory counts

46

as evidence for the occurrence of a waking event, so also, unless some good reason to the contrary is forthcoming, it counts as evidence—suitably modified of course by other evidence—for the occurrence of sleeping events. Hence Malcolm's verification requirement is, in fact, supplied.

It may be wondered whether Malcolm has overlooked the possibility of this reply, based on memory, to his verification argument. He has not, in fact, overlooked it, at least not completely. On p. 42, in considering how a man could know that a certain judgment occurred while he was dreaming, he notes that the man might say, ' "I distinctly recall that I came to that conclusion about Smith at the same time I was having a dream" '. 'But now,' Malcolm replies, 'we have to put the previous question, namely, what could possibly verify this impression of his as true? Clearly nothing could.' But in saying this Malcolm is denying that the 'distinct recall' of the man is verification. And if we deny this, what right have we to accept 'distinct recall' as a verification in other contexts? 'I *know* I have been in your hotel before because I distinctly recall writing a remark in the visitors' book.' Such a recollection would usually be regarded as an adequate verification.

I can think of one reply to this argument. You can check your recall in the case of the hotel, it might be said, by looking at the visitors' book, but you cannot do that for a dream. This reply, however, will not do. There are many non-dreaming events we claim to recall which are not checkable in this way. For example, we say, 'I remember thinking what a good day it would be for a walk in the mountains'; or, 'I was lost in a day-dream: I was picturing what the new town hall will be like'. To both these cases we could apply Malcolm's rhetorical question and its answer: 'But now, we have to put the previous question, namely, what could possibly verify this impression of his as true? Clearly nothing could.' Nothing, that is, except the fact that, in both cases, I remember what I claim to have happened. And this remembering is in fact accepted as a verification of my claim. If such verification were not accepted, our daily commerce with one another would be greatly altered. We should accept recollections of the visitors'-book variety where public verification is possible, but we should look askance at such statements as, I remember noticing that the safe door was closed at 6 p.m. last night (though it is open now). What is there to verify my claim to have noticed that the door was closed? Noticing leaves no finger-prints. Even if I had written down my noticing in a diary, the worth of the entry would depend on the worth of my recollection as I wrote it down. And if the view we are considering is correct, that latter worth is just nil.

Assuming then that we do accept as evidential such recollections as, I remember noticing, or, I remember day-dreaming, despite the absence of independent verification, then the lack of independent verification cannot be consistently used as an argument against accepting as evidential such recollections as, 'I had a nightmare last night'.

But, Malcolm might still reply, there is a difference—and it is a big difference—between remembering a dream and re-membering a day-dream. In the latter case you are awake, but in the former you are asleep. Now, it is not to be denied, he might say, that day-dreaming occurs. You can be aware you are day-dreaming. But when you are asleep you cannot *ipso facto* be aware of anything. A man can no more be aware of anything when he is asleep than, to use Malcolm's comparison, a man can be aware of anything when he is dead.

But now, is it so obvious, we must ask in response, that a man cannot be aware of things when he is dead? Was Virgil's Dido not aware of Aeneas? The *Aeneid* may be false, but it is not senseless. No more is Dante a nonsense-monger. Nor is Bunyan. Being aware when one is asleep might therefore have sense so far as this comparison with being dead is concerned. And what other reason can be given for holding that we can-not be aware when we are asleep? I cannot see that any other reason is given. Malcolm states that 'if a man can assert "I am asleep" he is *ipso facto* not asleep'; but what support is there for this statement? If appeal is made to the impossibility of verification then we can reply that memory, as we have argued, does supply the required verification. That memory does do so can only be denied by appealing to the premiss that mental events cannot occur during sleep. And this premiss, as we have just seen, we can reasonably refuse to accept.

So far, then, as considerations of verification, meaning, good sense or logic are concerned we may continue to think of dreams as experiences occurring while we are asleep. Logic, to adapt Lewis Carroll's statement, will not stop us doing so. In other words, we must regard the story theory in its logical form as unproven. I do not say, however, that we have disproved the view. If we are prepared to be sufficiently, or discriminatingly, sceptical concerning memory then the theory might still be acceptable. But do we wish to pay this price? This is a point to which I shall return towards the end of this chapter.

The story theory (factual form)

But we have still to reckon with the story theory in its factual form. Dreams, as experiences while asleep, could possibly occur, it will be said, but as a matter of fact they do not; or, at least, the facts can be perfectly well explained by supposing they do not.

As we noted at the outset of this chapter it is not easy to find a detailed statement and defence of the factual story theory. The grounds on which we might adopt the theory are presumably as follows: (a) experiences while asleep are possible, i.e. the logical form of the story theory is untrue, but (b) the evidence for such experiences is inadequate and (c) economy therefore requires that if possible we account for dreams on some hypothesis other than the occurrence of experiences while asleep.

The factual story theory would be based mainly therefore on requirements of scientific method: adequacy of evidence and economy of hypothesis. The theory, we note, affirms what

49

the logical story theory denies, namely that experiences during sleep are possible. The two forms of the story theory are therefore incompatible. Hence it is not surprising to find that Malcolm, as champion of the logical theory, considers that the factual theory must 'result from confusion' (p. 58).

What then are we to say of the factual theory? It claims, as we have seen, to have science on its side. But there are certain formidable objections to it. Of these I shall keep the most telling to the end. There are, to begin with, the quite serious objections which we noted already, but which Malcolm, in accordance with his view that experiences cannot happen during sleep, was bound to disallow. There is the continuity objection: you awake terrified after, it seems, the terror of a bad dream. The one terror seems to be the continuation of the other—if indeed one can divide the terror at all. Perhaps you cried out in apparent fear while still asleep. Surely it is very implausible to deny that you were in fact terrified while asleep. The answer which Malcolm gave to this objection might be adopted by the factual story theorist: you feel terrified when you awake because you are under the impression that you have had a terrifying experience. But, we might reply, is this in fact why you feel terrified? I must leave the reader to decide.

Then there is the asthmatic objection: the patient dreams he is feeling suffocated and is in fact being suffocated. How can we deny that his dream-feeling occurs along with his physical discomfort, i.e. during sleep? Malcolm again provided an answer to this objection: if the patient is really suffocating then he is not asleep, at least not sound asleep; but dreams occur only when we are sound asleep; therefore the patient could not have dreamt.

But this argument proves too much. Suppose a man awakes declaring that he has had a frightening dream and suppose also that his adrenalin gland was secreting fluid just as it would if he were awake, then would we not have to say that the man was therefore not sound asleep? Or suppose the man dreamt that he was cold and his toes were in fact exposed, then . . . On this line of argument it would be very hard to find a sleeping man at all.

This matter of being sound asleep and not sound asleep draws attention to a curious feature of the story theory (in either form). A man falling asleep goes gradually from a state of being awake through one of dozing till he is finally sound asleep. Now it is allowed that he may have experiences, e.g. mental imagery, right up to the point at which he becomes sound asleep. But when he passes the frontier between being almost sound asleep and being quite sound asleep he no longer, according to the story theory, has experiences. But can we find this frontier on one side of which experiences occur, on the other side of which they do not? I do not think so. Perhaps it will be said in reply, No—there is no frontier; you pass gradually from being half-asleep to being sound asleep; but when you are sound asleep your state is *toto coelo* different from that of being half-awake. But the difficulty will then be this. When you are half-asleep experiences occur; when you sound asleep they do not. What is the situation half-way between these two states? Experiences cannot half-occur. We are driven back to the theory of a clear-cut frontier, but a clear-cut frontier we cannot find.

Other objections to the factual form of the story theory may be briefly mentioned. When we awake after a dream, we usually consider that the dream-events have just occurred— shortly before we woke up, i.e. during sleep. Malcolm's answer to this was that such a dating is too vague to fix the alleged dream-events in physical time. But, we can reply, do we not constantly accept dating of equal vagueness in waking life? It happened a few hours ago, we say; or, I saw him sometime in the last few days; I was day-dreaming of our trip to Panama just now.

Another objection we had noted to the story theory in its logical form was an argument from physiology. If brain change B is associated with mental change J in waking life then if B

51

occurs when we are asleep may we not conclude that J is also occurring, and particularly so if the subject records that he did have a J-ish dream? The story theorist might reply to this, as Malcolm in fact does, that the correlation could be explained as existing between bodily experience J and dream *record,* that the correlation does not require us to postulate any experience while asleep. I think this reply must be considered valid. The physiological argument alone would not refute the story theory. But granted some more powerful objections, e.g. the objection from continuity, the physiological objection can be a useful ally.

I have kept to the end, however, the most telling objection to the factual story theory. This is the main point we urged against the logical story theory, namely that to refuse to grant that experiences occur while asleep is to discredit memory in a gratuitous manner. We awake and vividly recall experiences we think we have had just now. If we refuse to grant that this vivid recall provides a good reason for believing that the recalled events occurred why should we give credence to vivid recall in other contexts? Why should we, for example, accept a child's recollection of his day-dream? The child tells he is frightened because he has just had a realistic day-dream of a menacing robber; we do not tell him that he has had no experience. We tell him he only imagined it. Why should we treat his night dreams differently?

I conclude, therefore, that the story theory in both its forms is open to serious objection, the main objection against it in either form being that it implies an unwarranted distrust of memory.

We must indeed concede that this objection though formidable is not conclusive. We could, it must be granted, take the view that the evidence of memory may be relied on when it concerns waking events but is to be given no credence when it refers to events alleged to occur during sleep. We could take this view, and we could not be dislodged by logic. But, as the example we took of the sleeping child shows, we should certainly not have the plain man on our side—not to mention the fairly imposing list of philosophers whom Malcolm quotes as having erred. And, it might be urged, if we are to reject the view of the plain man, a view which has so far survived, then the onus of proof lies on us. Why should we reject that view? Malcolm's verification reasons we have not found to be adequate. Economy is a possible reason, but we should be buying economy at the price of complexity. Instead of a homogeneous theory of memory-belief we should be substituting a more complex view: trust memory here, but don't trust it there. Granted then that the onus of proof for rejecting the plain man's view of dreams would rest on us it does not appear that the case we could offer would carry much conviction, except with a man who greatly preferred the economical to the simple.

Assuming, then, that we have found no good reason for departing from the plain man's view of dreams, what does that view come to? At the beginning of this chapter we noted that in common speech we use 'I never dreamt of such a thing', as equivalent to 'I never imagined such a thing'. And we saw that to the child frightened by a nightmare we may say, 'It was only imagination'. Dreaming, common usage suggests, may be treated as a species of imagining. The only question is, what species?

I have already suggested that the answer is supposal. When we dream of seeing Buttermere we are not seeing Buttermere 'in imagination'—that would be a day-dream; nor are we seeing Buttermere 'with imagination'—we should then be practising, or on the way to practising, the arts of poetry or painting. Rather we are supposing that we see Buttermere. Dreams in this respect resemble illusions. I imagined I was looking down a corridor (but it was a mirror)=I supposed I was looking down a corridor. The main difference is that in the case of the illusion we are awake, whereas the dreamer is asleep.

There is another possible difference. The illusion is a case not only of supposal but of false supposal. Are all dreams likewise cases of false supposal? What about the veridical dream? I am thinking of such cases as that of the asthmatic sufferer, who dreams he is suffocating and is in fact suffocating. Or, more commonly, there is the man who dreams he is falling and is in fact falling. I am not sure however that these are, normally at least, genuine exceptions. The man who dreams he is falling rarely dreams he is falling out of bed. He usually believes he is doing something much more adventurous and dangerous, slipping from a scaffolding or stumbling over a cliff. The suffocating feeling of the asthmatic patient may usually be transmuted likewise. There is also a nicer point. To be falling out of bed is not only to be changing the position of one's body in a downward direction: it is also to be feeling certain sensations and emotions. Now since the dreamer is asleep then presumably, even if he is in fact falling out of bed, he is not experiencing the same sensations and emotions as he would experience if he were awake and falling out of bed. So even if he dreamt he was falling out of bed, i.e. believed in his dream that he was falling out of bed, he would still be believing falsely; for the event falling-out-of-bed in, as it were, its fullness, is not in fact occurring: the appropriate sensations and emotions are not taking place.

A similar observation applies to the asthmatic case. It may be that in the sleeping patient the physical conditions of suffocation are occurring; but there is no reason to think that exactly the same sensations as he would experience when awake are occurring. Hence if he believes, in his dream, that he is suffocating, his belief is still a false one. It is only dream-suffocating, together, as it happens, with certain physical events, that is occurring: suffocating in its fullness is not doing so.

These apparent exceptions to our conclusion that in a dream we are falsely supposing are, not therefore, genuine. There is, however, another possible type of dream which we should

54

consider. The type we have just examined is that in which we dream we are having an experience—falling, suffocating or whatever it may be. But we might also have a dream of a more impersonal kind, e.g. that Australia has won the Test Match. We wake up, turn on the wireless, and the announcer confirms our dream. In this case it can hardly be denied that what we believed, in its fullness, was true—granted of course that our dream did not occur before the match was in fact won. Hence in this dream we could not be said to have falsely supposed. We may have believed without evidence, and believing-in-a-dream may well be different emotionally and conatively from believing when awake, but what we believed, is certainly, in this case, the truth. We must therefore qualify our previous conclusion and say that most dreams are instances of false supposal. But some dreams are cases of supposal plain.

VI

DREAMS—WHAT THEY PROVE

My object in this chapter is to consider three connected questions that have been much discussed of late. These questions have their origin in the passage in Descartes' *Meditations* already referred to in the last chapter. In this passage Descartes poses what we may call his dream-problem. And this problem, which we shall be shortly considering, has given rise to the questions we are to discuss: (1) Was it nonsensical of Descartes to look for a 'certain mark' to distinguish sleeping from waking? (2) Do we know that we are now awake? and (3) If we know that we are now awake, how do we know? The three questions have a connection. If we answer the first in the affirmative, i.e. if we decide that no 'certain mark' can be found, and if we are convinced, as we are likely to be convinced, that we are now awake, then we may well be inclined to answer the third question by saying that when we are awake we just know we are awake—that is all there is to it. We don't know we are awake by any mark, we just know. The waking state, as is sometimes said, is self-authenticating.

I shall be arguing that in fact the answer to the first of these questions is, No. Descartes was not engaged in a foolish quest, whatever we may think of the 'marks' he eventually offered. My answers to the second and third questions would take longer to state, and had better be deferred to the appropriate point in the discussion.

Descartes' dream problem is briefly this. As the philosopher sits in his dressing-gown beside his fire, it occurs to him that during sleep he has often had experiences like those he is now having. Still there is no doubt that he is awake now. But when he looks for some mark that will enable him to distinguish between sleeping and waking he cannot find any. And this puzzles him immensely—so much so that he can almost persuade himself he is now dreaming.

However, as his readers know, there is a happy ending to the *Meditations*. Descartes manages to re-build his house— even if there is a little uncertainty about the upper storeys and the roof. And he finds that all his previous doubts should be rejected as 'hyperbolical and ridiculous, especially the general uncertainty respecting sleep, which I could not distinguish from the waking state: for I now find a very marked difference between the two states, in respect that our memory can never connect our dreams with each other and with the course of life, in the way it is in the habit of doing with events that occur when we are awake. And, in truth, if some one, when I am awake, appeared to me all of a sudden and as suddenly disappeared, as do the images I see in sleep, so that I could not observe either whence he came or whither he went, I should not without reason esteem it either a spectre or phantom formed in my brain, rather than a real man. But when I perceive objects with regard to which I can distinctly determine both the place whence they come, and that in which they are, and the time at which they appear to me, and when, without interruption, I can connect the perception I have of them with the whole of the other parts of my life, I am perfectly sure that what I thus perceive occurs while I am awake and not during sleep'.[1]

The following features of Descartes' account deserve special notice.

(1) He takes it as obvious that he has had experiences—lifelike experiences—in his dreams.

(2) He eventually offers two criteria to distinguish waking from dreaming experiences. The two criteria are (a) coherence and (b) distinctness in space and time.

By way of contrast to this account which Descartes gives of

[1] Everyman's edition, p. 142.

his problem let us see how that problem is dealt with by Professor Malcolm in his recent book referred to in the last chapter. He does not, we may note at the outset, give quite the same account as we have done of what Descartes says, for he attributes to Descartes only one 'mark', namely, coherence. This point of interpretation is not a minor matter: that Descartes should not have confined himself to coherence is, I shall be arguing, of some importance.

Leaving aside, however, for the moment this point of interpretation let us see how Malcolm answers Descartes' problem. He begins with a radical criticism of coherence as a 'mark'. If you want to know whether you are awake or dreaming then coherence is of no use to you because you might be only dreaming your experience was coherent (p. 108). In any case, the question, Am I dreaming? is senseless, because it presupposes, or implies, the question, Am I asleep? and this is not, Malcolm considers, a question that can be sensibly asked (p. 109). In short, coherence is for him a useless answer to a pseudo-question. In looking for a mark to distinguish waking from dreaming experience Descartes was wasting his time.

We may expect that Malcolm will in consequence give short shrift to the question, Do we know, or only believe, that we are awake? There is, he has argued, no question as to whether we are awake. This fact we may, if we like, signify by saying, We know we are awake, but strictly, the phrase 'we know' is here redundant: 'we know we are awake' means no more than 'we are awake'. We just are awake, and that is the answer to Descartes (Chapter 18).

Descartes has therefore, if Malcolm is right, returned a useless answer to a bogus question. Let us leave aside the matter of Descartes' answer, and consider first Malcolm's case against Descartes' question. This case rests on the proposition that we cannot sensibly ask the question, Am I asleep? And this proposition is an instance of Malcolm's general conclusion that no experience of any kind can occur during sleep. But this general conclusion we examined and rejected in the last

58

chapter. It follows that, so far as Malcolm's argument goes, Descartes' problem remains. There is, so far as anything has been proved to the contrary, a real question, What mark or marks distinguish waking from dreaming experience? And there are the real questions, Do we know for certain that we are now awake? and, If so, how do we know?

Granted then that Descartes' problem has not been ruled out of order what can we contribute towards its solution? In the remainder of this chapter I propose to approach the problem concerned not by a direct assault but rather by what I might call the back-door. I intend to generalize two problems well-known in the history of philosophy and to use them so generalized to confirm the reality of Descartes' problem and to assist towards its solution.

The first of these problems was proposed by William Molyneux. The second is a question raised by Hume.

Molyneux's problem

William Molyneux, F.R.S. (1656-1698), correspondent of Locke and author of *Dioptrica Nova,* a book on optics studied by Berkeley, introduced Locke's *Essay* to Provost Ashe of Trinity College, Dublin, who had it prescribed for Bachelors in the college to read.[1] The second edition of the *Essay* (1694) contains Molyneux's problem, the passage concerned running as follows:[2]

'To which purpose I shall here insert a problem of that very ingenious and studious promoter of real knowledge, the learned and worthy Mr. Molineux, which he was pleased to send me in a letter some months since: and it is this: "Suppose a man born blind, and now adult, and taught by his touch to distinguish between a cube and a sphere of the same metal, and nighly of the same bigness, so as to tell, when he felt one

---

[1] See the letter of Molyneux to Locke, dated December 22, 1692, in *Some Familiar Letters between Mr Locke and Several of His Friends,* London, 1708.
[2] Locke, *An Essay Concerning Human Understanding,* ed. Fraser, Vol i, pp. 186 f; Everyman ed., pp. 52 f.

and the other, which is the cube, which the sphere. Suppose then the cube and sphere placed on a table, and the blind man to be made to see; query, Whether by his sight, before he touched them, he could now distinguish and tell which is the globe, which the cube?" To which the acute and judicious proposer answers: "Not. For though he has obtained the experience of how a globe, how a cube, affects his touch; yet he has not yet attained the experience, that what affects his touch so or so, must affect his sight so or so; or that a protuberant angle in the cube, that pressed his hand unequally, shall appear to his eye as it does in the cube." I agree with this thinking gentleman, whom I am proud to call my friend, in his answer to this his problem.'

Locke, as will be seen, endorsed Molyneux's answer to the problem. Berkeley, who also considered it, believed the problem would not have even made sense to the blind man because of the complete disparateness of sight and touch before experience.

Molyneux's problem can be regarded as a partial problem. It concerns a man deficient in one sense only. Suppose now that we were to generalize the problem. Let us consider the case of a man who because of a serious head injury becomes unconscious and remains so for months. Eventually, however, through the skill of a surgeon, he awakes from his long sleep. Let us make the following postulates:

1. He has been asleep so long that he has forgotten what it is like to be awake.

2. During his sleep he had dreams.

3. He has forgotten all events prior to his accident.

4. He has lost the power of recognizing such familiar objects as his home or his parents.

5. He does, however, retain the ability to recognize general objects, e.g. a man, a house. He will recognize his mother as a woman, though not as his mother.

These are not, I think, unreasonable postulates. Postulate 5 is required as a consequence of postulate 2: if he is to have dream-experiences he will need some equipment of general concepts. (The situation in which a man could recognize his mother as a woman but not as his mother I have put to a brain-surgeon and although he could not confirm its possibility from experience he considered that it might occur.)

The question I wish now to pose is this. Assuming that the man has become used to dreaming experience as the normal thing, how will his waking experience strike him? And in what way will he gradually re-learn the distinction between waking and dreaming life?

The original, special Molyneux problem, we remember, was this. Granted that a man has the use of four of his senses, can he extrapolate to the fifth? Our generalized problem is, Granted that the man has forgotten what sense-experience is like and has been accustomed only to the experience in imagination, i.e. he has the effective use of none of his senses, how will sense-experience strike him when he is restored to it again? In what way will he re-learn the distinction between waking and dreaming experience? The answer to this question I do not intend to discuss at this stage in any detail. Considerations relating to memory, vivacity of experience, coherence would enter. What I am concerned with rather is that the question itself—the generalized Molyneux problem—is not entirely fanciful: a man could be in the situation described, and it would make sense to say of him that he had to re-learn the distinction between waking and dreaming experience. And, we may add, as he does re-learn this distinction, he might well remark to himself—perhaps at an early stage of his recovery, 'I believe that I am now in the state called being awake; now what is it that makes me think so?' In other words, Descartes' problem would certainly be a real problem for him.

As the days go by the man would of course become so accustomed to what had been for him a novel experience—the experience of being awake—that he would no longer ask with any doubt in his voice, Am I awake? So likewise a man who

61

has only recently been introduced to a new taste, say the taste of olives, might at first have to query the experience, but before long he could recognize the fruit, with no doubt in his mind. He just knows it is an olive. Our former patient will also just know he is awake. But just knowing it is an olive does not exclude knowing it is an olive because of the peculiarities of its taste. So likewise the man may know he is awake because of some special features of his experience which he no longer needs to dwell on.

The inference I wish therefore to draw from the generalized Molyneux problem is this: there is a real question, How does waking experience differ from dreaming experience? The fact that this question may normally strike us as fanciful does not prove that it is a bogus problem; and, as we have seen, it could be a question of some moment to the man in the not impossible situation we have described. Nor does the fact that we just know we are awake rule out the possibility that we know we are awake because of certain features or Cartesian 'marks' of our experience. We may not need to dwell on these marks now, but that does not disprove their import for us. And the Molyneux man might well, as we have seen, recognize and use them more explicitly. Swiftness of recognition does not disprove aids to recognition.

Hume's problem

If the generalized Molyneux problem shows that there is a genuine question, How do waking and dreaming experiences differ?, Hume's problem generalized, I shall argue, indicates an answer to the question.

By Hume's problem I refer to his question in Book I, Part iv, Section 2, of his *Treatise,* 'What causes induce us to believe in body?'[1] He has just argued that there is no way of deciding whether the belief in body is true or false: Berkeley's arguments against unperceived existence neither carry conviction, nor can they be refuted. They are perfect examples of scep-

[1] S. 187, E.I. 183 [S=Selby-Bigge edition; E=Everyman edition.]

ticism.[1] The discussable matter, Hume considers is the cause of the belief.

It will be remembered that Hume divides the belief in question into two sub-beliefs. There is the belief in 'continued' existence and the belief in 'distinct' existence. He also shows how these beliefs appear in the thinking of the plain man— the 'vulgar'—and in the thinking of the philosopher. He argues that the belief in body, whether vulgar or philosophical, can be based neither on sense-experience nor on reasoning. The belief cannot be the result of reasoning; if it were, both the vulgar and philosophers should reach the same conclusion. In fact, they reach different conclusions: the vulgar believe that colours and sounds can exist unperceived; the philosophers do not.

Moreover the philosophers credit their unperceived existences with being the causes of their impressions, but—on Hume's principles—it is not by reasoning that we pass from effect to cause. Nor can the belief in question be the result of sense-experience. One element in the belief is the notion of 'distinctness'. To be distinct means to be not mind-dependent. Hence if one could see, hear or feel distinctness one ought to be able to see, hear or feel minds, which is not the case.

Hume deduces that since the belief in body cannot be the result of reasoning or sensation, it is therefore the product of imagination.

How does imagination produce the belief in body? Hume replies by pointing to certain facts—facts both about things and about us. About *things* we have the fact that our experience is 'constant' and that it is also coherent. As to *us*, there is the inertia of the imagination. These objective and subjective

---

[1] This was in 1739. Berkeley was 54, with 14 years of life still before him. He cannot be said to have lost an interest in philosophy, for *Siris* appeared in 1744. It is a curious thing that in his extant writings there is no reference to Hume. The fact may reflect both the intellectual isolation of a country diocese in Ireland and the tardiness with which Hume's ability as a philosopher came to be recognized.

causes between them, Hume argued ingeniously, produce the belief in body.

The plain man's belief he considers to be absurd, because it assumes unperceived perceptions. The philosopher's belief is not much better, being the 'monstrous offspring of imagination and reason'—an attempt by reason to solve a problem created by a non-rational faculty, imagination.

Let us now consider how Hume's problem could be generalized. Let us suppose that a man's experience has become, for some reason, crazy—crazy in the respect that neither of Hume's objective features are exhibited by it. He looks out of the window and sees a church: he looks away from it, then looks back again—but it is gone. Or, to take another case, he puts his kettle on the gas, goes away and comes back expecting the kettle to be boiling; but, alas, it is still cold. And so on. His world has ceased to display constancy and it has ceased to be coherent. As a result the man will, assuming that Hume's theory is in general on the right lines, cease or begin to cease to have his belief in body.

Though the man will have lost, or be on his way to losing his belief in body, he will still, we may reasonably assume, believe that his experiences, though crazy, are really happening. He may toy with, but will probably reject, the suggestion that this is all a bad dream. Thus he has retained the distinction between the real and the imaginary. His present experiences, though crazy, lie on the real side of the line.

Here we have a clue to the generalizing of Hume's problem. Hume's problem—his special problem—is, What causes us to believe in body? The generalized problem will be, What causes us to believe in reality?

In dealing with this question we may follow the Humian pattern. We shall distinguish between the vulgar and the philosophers. It is often remarked that, whatever the argument from illusion may be worth, at least it draws our attention to certain facts we, *qua* vulgar, tend either not to notice, or else to ignore. The vulgar, we shall assume, believe that all their waking experiences are real, but that their dreams are unreal. The philosophers, who know a little better, agree that dreams are unreal, but point out that not all waking experiences are real: hallucinations, for example, must be put on the unreal side of the line.

Both vulgar and philosophers then draw the line between the real and the unreal, though they draw it in different places. The Humian question then is, What causes them to draw the distinction? The candidates will again be our senses, our reason and our imagination. It cannot be our senses that provide the distinction. Obviously it cannot be a man's eyes, nor his nose, that will cause him to regard a dream as unreal. Nor can it be reason that provides the distinction, because, if it were, the vulgar and the philosophers would not draw the line in different places. (We noticed that Hume gave as an additional argument against reason in the case of the belief in body, that we cannot reason from a perception to its cause, i.e. to body, the causal relation being always a matter of fact, not logic. I am not sure that he would want to apply that argument in the case of the real and the imaginary, because he does hold that we can argue from ideas to impressions, since we know the principle 'All ideas are derived from impressions'; but, of course, how we can know this universal proposition is not at all clear.)

Since neither sense nor reason will give us what we want, it must be the remaining candidate, imagination, that does so.

How, then, does imagination provide the distinction between the real and the unreal? The answer, following Humian lines, may again be found in objective and subjective facts—that is, facts of our experience and facts about us.

First our experience. Here we would naturally begin with the Humian feature, vivacity. For Hume, a vivacious perception, i.e. a perception with a strong degree of vivacity, is a perception we believe in: e.g. I believe that this hard surface is there, that it is real. (There is, indeed, Hume would prob-

65

E

ably concede, no necessity about this—we might have believed our vivacious perceptions to be imaginary and our weak perceptions to be real.)

In his discussion of the belief in body Hume confessed that constancy alone will not explain the belief. As a result he finds that he and his readers must pursue a 'considerable compass of very profound reasoning', a prospect not altogether displeasing to the author. In the case of the belief in reality likewise we have to remark that vivacity alone is not enough. For dreams are vivacious and yet they are treated—both by the vulgar and philosophers—as unreal. We need a second feature of experience to explain our rejection of them. This second feature could be the Cartesian mark of coherence. We need not decide here whether Humian vivacity and Cartesian coherence are the whole story, but we may note that coherence alone, like vivacity alone, is an insufficient criterion. One could imagine a set of dreams occurring on successive nights which were coherent with one another and with the events of waking life.

Thus by generalizing Hume's problem we have arrived again at Descartes' problem, and we have been led to notice two objective criteria in answer to it. But a Humian treatment would not stop there. Hume would presumably ask, Why is it that we regard the vivacious and coherent as real? i.e., What is the subjective factor that makes our imagination react in that way? Presumably Hume should again, as in the case of body, appeal to the inertia of the imagination. It is not difficult to link inertia with one of our two objective criteria, namely, coherence. We may recall Hume's example of the porter bringing him a letter. Hume might have assumed that the porter had suddenly appeared in the room, as it were *ex nihilo*. But he prefers to assume, to imagine, that the porter came up the unseen stairs. So also with our dreams. We dream we have been to Tokyo. Now we might assume that we have in fact been there and back in five minutes, but this would require our imagination to leave its well-worn grooves, and

66

so we reject the suggestion. Thus Hume would appear as a defender of the coherence theory of reality.

How does the imagination work in relation to our other objective criterion—vivacity? To begin with, I suppose we might say that there is no necessity about the fact that we take the vivacious to be real. We do, in fact, as we have seen, reject the vivacious dream. I think we should then need to recognize another feature of imagination. Not only does it display inertia, it also exhibits what we might call credulity. Being as it were assaulted by the vivacious perception, we are not hard-headed enough to resist and we concede reality to our assailant. Thus we take dreams to be real at the time of their occurrence, even though coherence together with inertia may lead us later to regard them as unreal.

This Humian approach to Descartes' problem provides an answer, or at least a comment, on what might have looked like an unanswerable remark by Malcolm that we noted above. Coherence is no good, Malcolm remarked, as a means of telling us whether we are awake or dreaming—because we might be only dreaming our experience is coherent. True, Hume might say. It is just the same with body. Nobody can prove body, nor disprove it. But, nevertheless, there remains the question, What causes induce us to believe in body? And Hume would claim that he has given them—constancy, coherence and inertia. You, he might say to us, in like manner may not, by generalizing my problem, have found any way of proving or disproving that you are awake. But what you may have found is the answer to the question, What causes you to believe you are awake? The answer consists in vivacity and coherence on the side of the object, inertia and credulity on the side of the subject.

As we know, there are a number of alternatives to the Humian theory of 'body', varying from the sophistication of Kant's categories to the bluntness of the plain man who just knows that there is a body—that his unfelt money is now in his pocket, that the mill-stream continues to flow unheard. But it can be reasonably argued that however assured Kant or the plain man may be it is still possible that both are mistaken: the money may in fact only exist when it is felt, the stream when it is heard. The sceptic, as Hume argued, cannot here be finally disproved. And Hume's account of *why* we believe in body may therefore still have application.

In the same way there are alternatives to a Humian treatment of the belief that we are awake. There could be a Kantian account, which it would not be hard to develop, and there is the plain man's view that of course we know we are awake: the state of being awake, as a philosopher might put it, is self-authenticating. But again, it can be reasonably argued that both Kant and the plain man may be mistaken. Their experience *might* be just as it is now and yet the whole thing be a dream. 'She hoped (fancifully, no doubt, but absolutely so?) that this was all a bad dream from which she would soon awake.' The sceptic, here also, cannot be finally disproved. And a Humian account of *why* we believe we are awake might therefore still be useful.

To conclude, I have used the generalized Molyneux problem to show that there is a real question, What are the differences between waking and sleeping experience? I have used the generalized Hume problem to show that the conviction that we are awake need not be self-authenticating: the conviction, if I am right, might be created by the causes we have discerned. Being the creatures we are, and having the kind of experience we do have we cannot help believing that we are awake, but the existence of this strong belief does not prove that its truth is beyond question.

In our discussion of dreams, in this and the previous chapter, we have amongst other things defended the view that the dreamer is a man who imagines, i.e. supposes, usually falsely. But we have not paid much attention to what he supposes. What he supposes is that the experiences he is having are real.

But, as we know, they are not real. They consist, we should usually say, of imagery. So likewise, we should say, the experience of the day-dreamer is that of imagery. Now imagery has been a subject of controversy in recent years. The term 'mental image' in particular has been under heavy fire. I propose in the next chapter to consider whether this term is one we should dispense with or retain.

VII

IMAGES

The word 'image' suggests the visual, and the various types of image discussed by philosophers and psychologists—mirror-images, after-images, memory-images, imagination-images—are usually considered with reference to sight. Ordinary language agrees with this practice. 'Visualize' is a common or garden word. The *Oxford English Dictionary* records neither 'auralize' nor 'tactualize'.

This stress on the visual has given a handle to those who for one reason or another are ill-disposed to imagery. Perhaps impotent to visualize themselves, they write off 'mental images' in any form. Or they find Hume's cardinal defect to lie in his being a 'visualizer'. If he had paid more attention, it is said, to touch and movement, he might have reached different conclusions.

It is possible that there is something in the critics' case. Whereas 'mirror-image' is a harmless term, whose application is easy to verify, 'mental image' is a term of theory, and possibly a theory of limited validity. It may be useful, therefore, to take account of the experience of a blind man—blind from birth. How far would he be inclined to use the image-terminology? The word 'image' is a noun and it might be thought that his experience would lend itself more readily to verbs: he is aware of happenings, rather than of things.

Let us suppose that the blind man, an inhabitant of Trinity College, Dublin, hears (or feels on Braille) the phrase 'Front Square'. Now the Front Square is for him, we may suppose, a place a hundred or more paces across, a place where the ground is for the most part cobbled. Sounds have there a special quality, different from those of a street or a field. The air-currents swirl in a distinctive way. The Front Square is, then, the place where you receive sounds and feels of a special quality and where you can walk with such and such degrees of freedom.

But a refinement is needed. If a sighted man stands in the Front Square he will, provided his eyes are open and it is daylight, see the square. The blind man may stand there, and if there happens to be no sound, or if his ears are out of action, or if the air is still or if he does not move around, he will have little or no clue as to where he is. We might be inclined, therefore, to contrast the two men's experiences by calling one categorical and the other hypothetical. The sighted man just sees what is there; whereas of the blind man we must rather say that if he moves, or shouts, or walks, he will have such and such experiences; in other words such and such events will occur to him. If this way of describing their two sets of experiences is accurate then the Front Square for the blind man will be a complex of events, whereas for the sighted man it is a *thing*. It would follow that the blind man's imagining might be similarly different from that of the sighted man.

It might be objected that this contrast is too sharp. The blind man's conception of the Front Square is built up from experiences had when there were, in fact, sounds and air-currents. But so likewise the sighted man's conception is built up from observing it in daylight, i.e. when it can be seen. This is true; but it must be noted on the other hand that what the sighted man can see continues, so long as he keeps his eyes open, for twelve hours or more. The blind man's objects are much less continuous. Sometimes the wind is blowing, sometimes not. Sometimes there are sounds, sometimes not. Moreover the blind man will lack most of his touch-experiences unless he moves around; whereas the sighted man can have his experience, his view of the square without stirring—one view indeed, but reasonably embracing.

We have found, then, one fairly wide difference between the sensory experience of the sighted and the blind man and we have questioned whether there may not be a corresponding difference in their imagining. It could follow that a theory of sense-perception and a theory of imagination which were based on visual experience had to be qualified, perhaps severely, when other kinds of experience, particularly tactual and auditory, are taken into account. This possibility we shall now consider. Let us focus our discussion by using again a problem we considered in the last chapter, namely, the question about body raised by Hume, who, as we noted above has been attacked as a 'visualizer': 'What causes induce us to believe in body?' And Hume, as we saw, returns an answer in terms of constancy, coherence and the inertia of the imagination. Constancy: we look at the Front Square; we look away; we look back and have the same experience. Coherence: part of the Library is obscured from our view by the Campanile but we believe that this part is there.

The question now to be considered, the question of main interest to us, is this: Does the theory Hume has given lean too heavily on the sense of sight? How far, if at all, would the theory apply to the experience of the blind man? Would the blind man have, in fact, the belief in body which Hume has taken as his starting-point, the belief which his theory is constructed to explain? Let us see how far the blind man's experience is characterized by the two qualities Hume has distinguished, constancy and coherence.

Instances of constancy in the blind man's experience are easy to give. If he takes five paces from the door of his study he can invariably put his hand on his writing-table. Beside the table, to the left, he can feel his old leather arm-chair. Touch will also give him coherence. He knows well the surface of his table by feel, a familiar scratch here, a dent there. If a typewriter rests on his table so that it covers the dent, then when his hand moves along the surface of the table he finds that the series of touch-experiences continues in the accustomed way until he reaches the typewriter; the dent, however, is missing; but after his hand has passed the typewriter the series carries on as before. His experience here is analogous to that of the sighted man who is accustomed to see his study fire changing gradually from bright flame through red glow to grey ashes. If he leaves his study with the fire burning brightly and comes back in three hours' time he finds only ashes.

It follows then, that the blind man is offered the same, or similar, inducements, as is the sighted man, to believe in 'body', i.e. in the continued and distinct existence of material things. He will believe that his writing-table exists unfelt, and that the portion of its surface under the typewriter continues to exist.

Let us now look a little more closely at the content of the blind man's belief. What does he believe when he believes that part of the surface of his table exists under the type-writer? This, it will be remembered, is a question which Hume found to be answered by sighted men in two different ways, both of them highly unsatisfactory. The blind man, as an unreflective, plain man, one of Hume's 'vulgar', will believe, we may suppose, that there exists unfelt the experience he would have if he were to put his hand at the place on the table which his typewriter now occupies. At least we may say that this is what the plain blind man would believe by analogy with Hume's plain sighted man. Now this belief of the plain blind man is, according to Hume, absurd. A touch-experience cannot exist unfelt. An untouched touch-datum is a contradiction. Here the philosophers enter. They, to their credit, appreciate the contradiction, and to escape it they posit matter, that is, a second layer of existence. A reflective, i.e. philosophical, blind man would then, if Hume is right, agree that no unfelt touch experience exists under his typewriter. But something, he will believe, exists under it, and this something is matter. He will subscribe, therefore, to the theory of what Hume calls the 'two-fold existence of objects'.

Matter, as supposed by the philosophers, sighted or blind, has the two defining characteristics that Hume ascribed to 'body', i.e. it has a 'distinct' and 'continued' existence: it is independent of perception, and it continues to exist during the intervals when it is not being perceived.

To this theory of matter, however philosophical, Hume pays no more respect than he gave to the view of the vulgar. He calls it the 'monstrous offspring of reason and imagination'. It is reason which restrains the philosopher from accepting the self-contradictory vulgar belief in unfelt feels. But this negative role is the only one that reason can properly play. No reason can be given for the positive belief in matter. The blind man might, for instance, argue, 'My typewriter cannot rest on nothing, therefore there must be something, albeit unperceived, beneath it'. But this causal argument Hume would reject as unsound: causality is concerned only with experience; we cannot use it to argue to the unexperienced. He would conclude that the blind philosopher's belief in distinct and continued existence, no less than the vulgar belief, is a product of 'imagination', i.e. roughly, it is a belief not based on sensation, nor reached by inference.

Our study of the blind man's experience indicates, then, that his inability to see will not hinder him from passing through the stages of the process which Hume deplores. His experience will have the qualities of constancy and coherence, and presumably his mind will work rationally, and non-rationally, in a way similar to that of the sighted man.

We shall not enquire here how far Hume's analysis of the belief in body is sound—we shall be considering his views more critically in a later chapter—but we may notice here one further point of exposition. Hume's explanation of the sighted man's beliefs hinged, we saw, on the two qualities of constancy and coherence. These two qualities, Professor H. H. Price has argued, can be reduced to one, what he calls 'gap-indifference'.[1] Some series of experiences are such that if members of the series are missing, we ignore the gap. We

[1] H. H. Price, *Hume's Theory of the External World*, p. 60.

ignore the gap in our Front Square experiences and we ignore the gap in our view of the Library.

This notion of gap-indifference applies readily to the blind man's experience. He ignores the gap between a feel of his table at 6 p.m. and a feel at 11 p.m.; he also ignores the interruption made by his typewriter. Similarly, to take an example from another sense, he ignores the gap between hearing the sound of a stream at 11 p.m. and hearing the sound at 7 a.m.

Thus the sighted man turns a blind eye to the gaps in his seeing experiences. So, likewise, the blind man turns a deaf ear to the gaps in his hearing experiences, and ignores, likewise, the gaps in his feeling experiences. The sighted man believes or takes for granted that the grey granite persists unlooked at, because it persists when he does look at it. The blind man takes for granted that the sound of the brook persists when unheard.

Not all series are indeed of this kind. There are gaps which we do not ignore. The sighted man does not believe that the sun necessarily shone on the Library all the morning; nor does the blind man believe that the college bell was striking all the time he was absent.

The blind man and the sighted man then both have their broken series which they repair: the brook keeps babbling, the daylight remains. They both have their broken series which they do not repair: the bell is not always striking, nor the sun always shining. And, as Hume and Professor Price can show, reasons may be given in each case why these series are, or are not, repaired.

So far, then, as Hume's problem goes—a philosophical problem of some importance—we may conclude that it can be discussed indifferently in terms of the blind man's experience or the sighted man's experience. It does not look as if Hume, or other 'visualizer', will have gone seriously astray, in the case of this problem at least, by attending mainly to the sense of sight.

Having satisfied ourselves, then, with respect to the sensory experiences of the sighted and the blind man, let us now see how their imaginal experiences will compare. We may begin with after-imagery. The blind man takes off his hat, but he may still feel it on his head. It feels (or I feel), he might say, as if my hat were still on my head. The experience is thus located in space, the space of physical objects. This is one reason why it is sometimes considered that after-images are better called after-sensations. Another reason is this. The after-feel of the hat occurs without any effort on the blind man's part, and when the feel dies away he cannot revive it. In these respects it resembles a sensation and differs from a mental image.

The after-images of sight have like properties. I stare hard and long at a red cross on a green background and, on looking away, have an after-image of a green cross on a red background. This image is again located in space; it is seen on the table in front of me. Of course there is something odd about its location. For I can also locate it on the wall or the ceiling; or, if I close my eyes, 'see' it out in front of me. In fact it seems to be located in the direct line of my vision, wherever that may be directed. And when I see it on the table it does not seem to be part of the surface of the table, as an ink-blot splashed on the table would become. Rather, so far as I attend to the the after-image, the surface of the table tends to come out of focus. We might compare looking intently at one's face in a mirror as one shaves, or brushes one's teeth. If the mirror falls to the ground, you may experience a mild shock, caused by the sudden jolt to your focusing equipment. The swaying of a mirror in a boat can cause similar discomfort.

With the qualification just made, however, we can still say that the visual after-image is located, or localizable, in the space of physical objects. It shares also with the tactual after-image the property that its entrance and exit depend little on our volition. We see, therefore, why in this case also there

76

are reasons for preferring the term 'after-sensation' to the term 'after-image'. At the same time, partly because of the location peculiarity noted above, partly because of intrinsic properties of the object, it does not feel quite right to say, for example, that we *see* a green cross on the red background. The guarded formula, It is as if we were seeing a green cross . . . , fits the facts more closely. And if this formula raises the question, In what way 'as if'? a fair answer can be gathered from the facts of the example we have studied.

Let us pass now to the imagination-image. I can visualize my car parked where I left it in the Front Square. I have an impression of the Chapel nearby, the lawn in front and other objects. I can do this visualizing with my eyes open. The white paper in front of me becomes a blur, for I am not focusing on it, not looking at it. Indeed I tend to look away from nearby objects—out of the window, so that I may the more easily avoid focusing on them. Better still is to close my eyes. I can thus visualize the car and its neighbourhood with little or no distraction. Unlike the after-image case, what I am now aware of—the car-scene—is not located with reference to physical objects. I have no temptation to think that the scene I attend to as I stare unseeingly at the table is part of the table's surface. Moreover what I am aware of is to some extent at my behest. I say, I will picture my car—and the picture comes. I cease to attend to it and it disappears. The formula, It is as if I were really looking at my car, again fits the situation, but again the question arises, How 'as if'? Well, what I visualize is coloured; it has the right shape; it is like, more or less, what I would see if I were looking at my car. There are of course the extrinsic differences noted above, and there is the further not unimportant difference that my car is not in fact physically present to me so that I am not really looking at it.

Words are important here. The words 'the Chapel' are sub-vocally present to me along with the visual object, and with this object and the name a number of phrases begin to cross

the threshold of my attention—an eighteenth-century building, reverently conducted services, good singing. Such phrases
may produce incipient feelings—real feelings.

Consider now how the blind man might imagine the
Chapel. So far as feel goes he may have learnt to think of the
building as a place with five steps leading up to it and as
fronted by four pillars. How will he think of the four pillars,
and what will be his imagery? The sighted man can see the
four pillars at once, and when he pictures them he can visualize them together, side by side. The blind man is in some
contexts capable of a comparable experience, e.g. he can place
five fingers at one time on the notes of a piano, or he can
appreciate two, or more, simultaneous pin-pricks on his skin.
And the resulting imagery in these cases may yield co-existing
images of feel. But he cannot feel the four pillars of the
Chapel at once. He will hardly therefore have four feel-images
at once. Still, he will presumably succeed in thinking of the
four pillars as co-existing. What he will probably do is this:
he will have one feel-image which will assist him to think of
one solid continuing object, and he will be conscious that there
are four of these, i.e. four co-existing objects. So far as location
and control are concerned his experience will resemble that
of the sighted man. He will not locate his feel-image in the
space of real feels. And the entrance and exit of the feel-image
will depend on his will in a way that the after-feel of his hat
did not.

Some of these remarks on feel-imagery may strike a sighted
man as lacking a basis in fact, the reason being that sighted
people seldom experience clear-cut tactual imagery. Why they
do not is fairly obvious: the objects of sight are so en-
grossing that they leave comparatively little opportunity for
attention to the objects of other senses. Moreover there may
be a great deal of simultaneous tactual sensation—from the
hands, arms, legs—competing for attention. The blind man
learns to discriminate and attend to separate items in this mass;

the sighted man probably does not. Where there is no attention there is, as a rule, little or no consequent imagery.

The main features of after-images and imagination-images,
and the contrast between them, may now be summarized, as
follows:

After-images

(i) These are located with respect to our physical environment, e.g. an after-feel is located on the head, an after-sight in
the direct line of vision, wherever that may be directed.

(ii) Their appearance and disappearance is not subject to
our control.

(iii) Of them we are, sometimes at least, prepared to say,
'It is as if I were . . .' and we can add the relevant qualifications.

Imagination-images

(i) These are not located with respect to the physical environment. Where is the image, e.g. where in respect of this
room? only admits the answer, Nowhere. It is no more located
than is Erewhon or Lilliput.

(ii) These images usually require some effort for their
appearance and continued existence.

(iii) Of them we can say 'It is as if I were . . .', and can add
the suitable qualifications.

We are now in a position to remark also on the images in
dreams and in hallucinations.

Dream-images

These are not in fact located with respect to the subjects
round us, but in our dream we have little or no way of knowing this. If the Humian account of dreams we discussed in the
last chapter were correct, we could, indeed, decide that dream-
images are physically located. We could decide that we really
had been to Tokyo and had not merely fancied the journey.

The reason why we do not make this decision, according to the Humian account, is that it would cause us too much trouble: the inertia or laziness of our imagination saves the distinction between dreams and reality.

No effort is needed to summon or maintain dream-imagery —once we are asleep. We are unlikely in our dream to report 'It is as if . . .', though we might afterwards so report, in the past tense.

Hallucination-images

Examples are the delusions of the alcoholic, and some, if not all, ghostly appearances. Like after-images, these are located in space. They need not be in the direct line of vision. They are usually private to one observer. They can be sufficiently like what we see to pass for real objects. It may be only some external evidence—the absence of confirming data, the incompatibility of the appearance with known or accepted fact—that may arouse our suspicions.

The blind man can experience hallucinations—of sound, and no doubt of touch. He may hear what seems a voice—but no speaker can be found; or feel a touch, though it seems that nobody touched him. Privacy is not so useful a criterion for touch as for sight: touch-sensation, unlike visual sensation, is largely private.

Since it is possible to take a hallucination for a real experience, the experiences in hallucination must be pretty like those of sense: they are found, however, by the tests indicated, to be not sensations. The term 'image' is therefore appropriate.

We have then, studied the after-image, and the images which occur in imagination, dreams and hallucination. Our study shows that what leads us to assign a given image to any of these four classes is not some quality of the image itself, e.g. distinctness, but rather its relations to its environment, including the subject who observes it. These relations include those of space, time and privacy.

At the beginning of this chapter we noted divided opinions on the question whether images occur at all. Our answer to this question can now be given. After-images, we have seen, certainly occur: there are after-feels and after-sights. We do also visualize, and when we visualize there is something presented to us, something having the properties we have stated, and this is an image. So also for the experience of the blind man: when he tactualizes there is an object, and this is an image.

In affirming that images occur and in what sense they do so we are not of course saying that we cannot think without them. We might well answer the question, 'Where did you leave your car?' with the response, 'Beside the Chapel', and do little or no visualizing at all. Similarly for the blind man. But the fact that we sometimes think without images need not exclude our sometimes thinking with them.

Two current usages of the term 'image' we may note here in conclusion. There is the use in literary criticism, as in 'Shakespeare's sea-images'. Here image is roughly equivalent to comparison, or family of comparisons. Such literary images are not mental images. There is nothing imaginary, unreal about them. They are not merely 'in imagination'. Rather, we see the writer, in constructing them, acting 'with imagination'.

The other usage, frequent in contemporary journalism, is instanced in such phrases as 'The image of the British Labour party', 'The image of Russian foreign policy'. 'Image' here is near to 'conception'—the propositions that a word or phrase brings to mind—with the emotional overtones conveyed by a cognate term of 'imagination'.

In the second chapter we reached the conclusion that the term 'imagination' has three main usages, defined by the phrases 'in imagination', 'with imagination' and by the term 'suppose'. We have now considered the first and third of these and the connected topics of dreams and imagery. In the next two chapters we shall discuss the remaining usage.

VIII

WITH IMAGINATION

We now come to our third main usage of imagination—imagination as the power of invention, the source of originality. Three questions may be raised here:

1. What are the activities which can be performed with imagination?

2. What are the properties implied by the phrase 'with imagination'?

3. What causes something to be done with imagination?

Let us take our questions in order. Obviously painting, musical composition, and other fine art activities can be executed with imagination. But less fine arts admit the characteristic also. One can design clothes, play football or dance with, or without, imagination. Now these are all activities which allow some degree of freedom in the use of the relevant material. A waltz, a wedding-dress, or a football score can be executed or designed in a variety of ways. When we come to the craftsman, however, the situation is less clear. One is tempted to deny that the craftsman, so far as he is a craftsman, can work 'with imagination'. The tailor, it might seem, works only to the pattern he has been given; the cook keeps to her recipe. But sharp lines, here as elsewhere, may falsify—as the tailor or cook would be quick to point out. Both of them encounter the unforeseen, the unprovided for—and both, if they are to be efficient, must be ready to show invention. No relevant distinction of kind can be drawn between the plain cook and the chef: one wears a white hat, receives higher pay, and is more skilled and inventive than the other, but that is all. Admittedly a craftsman's work can, in part, be taken over by a machine—a cake-mixer, sewing machine or lathe.

82

But, in the case of most crafts, there is a residuum that demands an inventiveness which only the craftsman himself can supply.

The activities that can be performed with imagination are, then, activities that allow some freedom in the use of the relevant material. They need not, as we saw, be what are usually reckoned as artistic activities: the footballer and the cook can act with, or without, imagination.

The caricaturist provides a case worth study. Compared with a portrait painter his freedom is at once restricted and increased: it is increased in that he is allowed to exaggerate some feature that takes his fancy, restricted in that the way he exaggerates and the features he chooses are dictated or influenced by his aim—to amuse, instruct or satirize.

Our second question is, What are the properties implied by the phrase 'with imagination'? To answer this question let us take as an example an appreciation in a weekly newspaper of the Irish artist, Jack Yeats:[1] 'If an artist can exalt the everyday scenes of his native land so as to communicate the moods of drama, melancholy and boisterous high spirits, then surely we may judge him a rare imaginative spirit . . . Such titles as "The Whistle of a Jacket" and "Here comes the Chestnut Mare" remind us that Jack Yeats was also an imaginative writer.'

The first of the two judgments in this passage attributes to Yeats imagination in a high degree. The quality is shown in his ability as a painter to use the commonplace to communicate a variety of strong emotions. I suppose the term 'creation' might have been used as a synonym here.

The second judgment recognizes that he was also a writer with a good deal of invention in his work.

Creation and invention—the making of much out of little, of new structures out of old material—these seem to be the

[1] The *Observer*.

qualities the critic had in mind. These qualities, we may observe, can only be displayed by activities of the kind we noted in the answer to our first question—that is, activities allowing some degree of freedom to the performer.

We pass now to our third question.

What causes something to be done with imagination? Why is it that one artist's work displays imagination to a higher degree than does another?

There is, of course, a vast literature on this matter, treating of such topics as inspiration, incubation, genius. But the discussion is mainly psychological. And only a brief answer to the question is called for here.

Creation, we may say, is to some extent a matter of natural endowment, to some extent of deliberate endeavour. We can achieve novelty by conscious striving and preparation. But for outstanding success we need the kind of mind to which new patterns or successions of ideas, come with unusual ease. Presumably the latter gift was Jack Yeats'; how far he would strain after novelty experts on his work may know. The preparation alluded to may take in part the shape of reading or observation. A well-stocked mind is in a good position to entertain novel trains of ideas. The novelty may indeed be more impressive to the unskilled observer than to the artist himself, who to some extent knows how the thing is done.

This brief consideration of the usage 'with imagination' will be supplemented by the discussion of the next chapter where it will be argued that when we relate art and imagination it is chiefly the usage 'with imagination' that is concerned.

IX

ART AND IMAGINATION

To judge by the selection of essays, *Aesthetics and Language,* any conjoining of art and imagination is at present suspect. Or, at least, we must not say that the work of art is a product of imagination, or an imaginary object. Thus Professor Gallie examines and rejects the idealist doctrine that 'Art is, essentially, Imagination',[1] that 'the true work of art is the internal picture' in the mind of its creator or of the spectator or reader.[2] Likewise Professor Passmore says, 'what Croce would have us believe is that whether we are contemplating architectural masses, or a Bach fugue . . . what we are in every case *really* contemplating is a certain form of human feeling.'[3]

Let us first, in the interests of accuracy, make sure that the doctrines here rejected are, or have been, in fact held.

The views of Croce form part of an idealistic metaphysic which not many would wish to support today. It will be more useful and fairer to the aesthetic position to be considered, if we look at it as stated in the writings of two authors less obviously committed to a general idealist position—R. G. Collingwood and Professor Susan Langer. Let us consider, first, a few statements from the former's *Principles of Art.* 'The artist finds expression for an emotion hitherto unexpressed' (p. 238). 'Art must be language' (p. 273). 'Imagination is the new form which feeling takes when transformed by the activity of consciousness' (p. 215). Imagination is 'tamed sensation'. The picture as seen by the spectator 'produces in him psychical

---

[1] *Aesthetics and Language,* ed. W. Elton, Oxford, Blackwell, 1954, p. 13.
[2] *Op. cit.,* p. 18.
[3] *Op. cit.,* p. 53. Prof. Passmore, of course, rejects Croce's view

experiences which . . . are transmuted into a total imaginative experience, identical with that of the painter' (p. 308).

And here are a few quotations from Professor Langer's writings. 'Art is the creation of forms [e.g. pictures] symbolic of human feelings' (p. 40). 'The picture is the Art symbol which expresses the imaginative experience, i.e. the artist's envisagement of feeling . . .' (p. 386f). 'The picture is . . . not the paint on the wall, but the illusion which Leonardo created by means of paint on damp plaster' (p. 387). These quotations are from her earlier book.[1] In her more recent work she writes, 'The Dance is an appearance; if you like, an apparition. It springs from what the dancers do, yet it is something else. In watching a dance you do not see what is physically before you — people running around or twisting their bodies; what you see is a display of interacting forces. . . .'[2] Or again, of painting she writes, 'A picture is made by deploying pigments on a piece of canvas, but the picture is not a pigment-and-canvas structure. The picture that emerges from the process is a structure of space, and the space itself is an emergent whole of shapes, visibly coloured volumes. Neither the space nor the things in it were in the room before. Pigments and canvas are not in the pictorial space; they are in the space of the room, as they were before, though we no longer find them there by sight without a great effort of attention. The picture, in short, is an apparition.'[3]

And about a work of art in general, 'A work of art is an expressive form created for our perception through sense or imagination, and what it expresses in human feeling'.[4] And of music: 'Sonorous moving forms . . . are the elements of music. The *materials* of music, on the other hand, are sounds of a certain pitch, loudness . . . I think the confusion between materials and elements is the crux of most difficulties in art theory. . . .'[5]

[1] S. Langer, *Feeling and Form*.
[2] S. Langer, *Problems of Art*, London, Routledge, 1957, p. 5.
[3] *Op. cit.*, p. 28.   [4] *Op. cit.*, p. 15.   [5] *Op. cit.*, p. 39.

The more important statements relevant to our topic made by Collingwood and Professor Langer—they would not necessarily both subscribe to all of these statements[1]—are as follows:

A picture is not paint on canvas but the illusion created by paint on canvas. Likewise for music and other works of art.

Spectator and artist can and should have the same 'total imaginative experience'.

A work of art is an expression, symbol or piece of language. What it expresses or symbolizes is human feeling.

What the writers in *Aesthetics and Language* allege has therefore a foundation. Two important contemporary writers do subscribe to the theses which Professor Gallie and his co-essayists reject. What assertions, we may now ask, would these latter writers make instead? Their position could be summed up in the following propositions:

The paint-on-canvas, they would say, is not merely the occasion for an imaginative construction, which is alleged to be the genuine work of art. The pigments, etc. do contribute to our enjoyment, and new materials have determined the direction of our inspiration (p. 6).

A picture is paint-on-canvas, a flat surface; it is also something that has depth. Both statements are true and can be seen to be so (pp. 7f).

There is no quality common to all works of art. At best we can talk of adopting an aesthetic attitude (p. 3).

It is pointless to talk of artist and spectator having the same imaginative experience. How could they know? (p. 5).

Music, for example, can be sad, but sadness is not something expressed by music. Sadness is in music as character is in a fact, or life in a squirrel (p. 5).

The main points of contrast here concern the following questions:

[1] Cf. *Feeling and Form*, pp. 380 ff. where Professor Langer defines the relation between her views and those of Collingwood.

What is in fact a work of art? How is it apprehended? What is its relation to feeling? What is its relation to imagination? These questions let us now consider.

What is a work of art? First, we must note that the term 'art' has a commendatory force. A particularly nice piece of safe-breaking might earn the compliment, It's a work of art. It has a finish, elegance, economy, ease which a rough, bull-dozing job will lack. Both jobs are the work of a craftsman, but the one shows artistry, the other not; and it is not hard to list as we have just done, the qualities that here mark the work of art. They qualify the way, the manner, in which the job is done.

Take now painting. Some painters are artists, others are not. The two-year-old doodler paints, but is not an artist. No more is the house-painter. A sign-writer might, however, claim to do artistic work. And a fond mother might hopefully declare of her child's drawing, Why, it's a work of art! The child has achieved either a success in representation, or an ability to produce striking patterns in colour, which lifts the picture out of the normal run of four-year-old efforts.

Similarly with music. The strummer provides noises, but lacks artistry. Only when she has acquired a reasonably good touch, a sense of rhythm, some degree of 'expression', can she be called a musician.

In many spheres of human activity then there is a line, though not necessarily a sharp line, of division. Above that line we have the artist; he is distinguished by certain marks, peculiar to his special activity, e.g. economy in the case of safe-breaking, a sense of colour harmony in painting, rhythm in music. Below the line we have the bungler, the inartistic, possibly even the good craftsman.

Artistic painting is then just superior painting—superior in fairly describable ways.

If this conclusion is correct, we may expect that there is unlikely to be a sharp distinction between the modes of being of art and non-art, and between the ways we apprehend each of these objects. In the case of a portrait, the poor likeness will tend to be non-art, the good likeness to be art. In both cases we see a likeness, with whatever this implies.

What then is the difference between looking at a real still-life and at a painted one? There might of course be no difference—i.e. if we were completely deceived by the painting—no difference, that is, in our state of mind. There would, of course, be the practical difference that in the one case there is something we could handle; perhaps even eat, in the other there is not. This difference is however irrelevant to aesthetics. If, then, we look at a real bowl of peaches, we may admire their lovely skin and complexion, we may praise the grower and wonder who he was. Our mouths may water in anticipation; we wonder whether we shall be offered one of the peaches, and if not how a hint might be delicately dropped. To the painted bowl of fruit our reactions are different. We may, or may not, wonder whether the picture is a good likeness; we may possibly speculate on the original: who was the fifteenth-century gardener who grew the fruit? how did he speak? and so on. But we shall probably also note and appraise the line and balance of the picture and its use of colour. We may, or may not, detect an attitude of affection for natural objects: only a lover of nature would have observed the way the leaf grows out of the stem . . . So our estimate is gradually built up; the picture is good in colour, excellent in line, poor in balance, shows a remarkable affection for nature. The estimate will be based on implicit comparisons. We have in mind some painting noted for its excellence of colour: the present picture fares not badly in the comparison.

As we judge we are, therefore, noticing, comparing, deciding. The success and worth of our estimate will depend on the sharpness of our perception, our knowledge, i.e. artistic experience, and our ability to make reliable comparisons.

So much for our apprehension of the picture. Now how do our emotions come into the matter? That is the next question we were to consider. The answer is that they may, or may not, do so. We may (or may not) be moved by the excellence of the line, or by sympathy with the artist's love of nature. The picture moved me, or did not move me: these are just additional judgments on it, not the only judgments, nor the sum-total of possible judgments. Emotion is not the focus of an aesthetic situation: it is just one element, a not indispensable element in the situation.

It may indeed be granted that pictures, and painters, differ greatly in this matter of feeling. Some painters, no doubt, paint under the stress of emotion, and what they paint and how they paint cannot be understood without reference to what they have felt or feel. No doubt van Gogh was excited at some stage when painting his sunflowers. And Stanley Spencer's village pictures convey an emotional intensity also. But these facts are too narrow a base for the general statement that art is the language of emotion. If it were, it would be a very uninformative language. In the English language, for instance, the word 'motor-car' always stands for the vehicle, and for nothing else. But take van Gogh's sunflowers. Such and such a use of colour may in this picture indicate, say strong affection. But there is no guarantee, indeed no likelihood, that the same line or colour will indicate a similar emotion in another painting, even by the same artist. This use of colour certainly went with that emotion on that occasion; we may even say that this artist's use of colour was an expression of what the artist felt, in the sense that it was the way he gave vent to his emotion.

In sculpture, music and other arts there may be likewise, in some cases, a reference to the artist's emotion. But, as we have stressed above, this fact does not make emotion a necessary element in every work of art, nor in those cases when the emotion is present is it necessarily the central element.

So much then for art and feeling. Let us now consider imagination. Collingwood, as we have noted, considers that spectator and artist should have the same 'total imaginative experience', and Professor Langer says that the 'picture is the art symbol which expresses the imaginative experience, i.e. the artist's envisagement of feeling', and that a 'work of art is an expressive form created for our perception through sense or imagination, and what it expresses is human feeling'.

Let us take an example. I am looking, let us say, at the portrait by Gainsborough of the 1st Duke of Bedford—a fine figure of a man. It is a work of art all right—it is a good painting by a good artist. I use my eyes to see it, but I do more than that: I see it as more than a pattern of colour: it is a copy of what the Duke of Bedford looked like to the artist. It is not, I know, a copy[1] of the Duke of Bedford. It is a copy of the look of the Duke of Bedford. (Compare Madame Tussard's exhibition where not only the look but the body of the subject is copied.)

In looking at the portrait there may not be much more exercise of imagination than in sense-perception. I have to be active, to some degree, in the latter case, if I am to see a pattern of colour as a bowl of fruit. So here I have to exert myself to see the pattern as a picture of the Duke of Bedford.

With abstract painting we may have to exert ourselves rather more. It is like seeing pictures in the fire. To see pictures in the fire we have to recognize a seen shape as like, or reasonably like, the shape of a house or a tree. What this requires of us is a gift of observation, a store of mental imagery and a readiness to see a likeness. Such equipment is possessed more richly by some men than others. So also with the abstract painting. We may have to find a likeness to a human body, and to find this we may need gifts of the kind just listed.

We may compare here what we found to be indicated by the phrase 'with imagination'. Freedom and originality are the two principal marks. So here to appraise the abstract paint-

---

[1] I know the word 'copy' sounds naive; I could have used 'likeness' or 'representation', but 'copy' is shorter.

ing the spectator needs flexibility; to produce the picture, the artist needed both flexibility and originality.[1]

What are we to say of Professor Langer's statement that a picture is '. . . a structure of space, and the space itself is an emergent whole of shapes, visibly coloured volumes'? Can we regard this as just a technical statement of the fact that to see the picture the spectator must, sometimes at least, discern a pattern? I cannot find more in it than this. Nor, I think, is there anything more we need discern in the case of the dancer. Here Professor Langer tells us that 'In watching a dance you do not see what is physically before you—people running around or twisting their bodies; what you see is a display of interacting forces. . . .' Certainly, in watching a ballet we may abstract, to some extent, from the human shapes, and allow our attention to be taken by the moving pattern of white colour. But I find it hard to agree that we do not see people moving around: their faces and limbs are still of some interest to us, and even if we closed our eyes to these, we should still be conscious that the makers of the pattern are human beings. If the pattern should suddenly break because one of the dancers has fallen with a crash, we react to the accident as being the fall of a human being, with all that this implies. It is not the fall of a robot, or a mere hiatus in a pattern of colour. Our disposition, our 'set', is towards a human being. And this disposition, with all that it implies, colours our experience throughout.

We saw above that the issue between Collingwood, Professor Langer and their critics turned on the question, What is a work of art? How is it apprehended? What is its relation to feeling? What is its relation to imagination? The answers we have reached to these questions are as follows.

[1] Professor Langer (*Feeling and Form*, p. 71n) refers to Leonardo who, 'in his *Treatise on Painting*, advises students to look at chance forms like cracks in plaster and knots in boards and try to make figures out of them, i.e. to read shapes of people and things into them. This, he says, is very good for the painter's imagination'. It is worth reflecting what Leonardo meant by 'imagination' here.

There is no sharp line between the work of art and the work of non-art. The difference is that between superior and inferior. The judgment, art or non-art, is made by reference to appropriate criteria—one set of criteria applies to safe-breaking, another to football, another to painting.

Since no sharp line can be drawn between art and non-art it is, we inferred, unlikely that they differ in their modes of being. If inartistic safe-breaking is a physical event, so is artistic burglary. If a child's doodling is lines on paper so is a drawing by Rembrandt.

On this first question, then, we have agreed with the *Aesthetics and Language* essayists rather than Collingwood and those who think like him. A picture is paint-on-canvas; an artistic picture is paint placed on canvas by an artist.

To answer our question about apprehension we compared our apprehension of a 'real' object with that of a painted one. What we found was a difference of reaction; we ask different questions, we pass different judgments. Thus in the former case it may be a peach's colour that we praise; in the latter it is the painter's use of colour to which we react. Again, we have agreed with the *Aesthetics and Language* writers.

Then as to feeling: we saw that when we look at or appraise a work of art our feelings may or may not be concerned. The picture or drama may, or may not, move us. Emotion is a possible ingredient of the situation: that is all. So also for the artist: he may paint coolly or he may paint under stress. Painters differ in temperament; and their own states of mind vary at different times.

Here also we find we cannot agree with the Collingwood type of theory which regards emotion as central and indispensable in artistic production and appraisal.

Finally, with regard to imagination, we saw that we may need to use our imagination, in varying degree, when looking at a work of art. We need to look with imagination: we need, that is, to be prepared to recognize unobvious likenesses, to abstract, and so on. But such activity on our part does not make the work of art an 'imaginary object', a product of imagination. So likewise, I cannot see Snowdon with my eyes shut. But I do not create it by opening them.

We have now considered the three main usages of the term 'imagination' we had distinguished and we have made some reference to the use of the term in recent philosophy. There are also two philosophers of the past in whose writings the term 'imagination' has a central place—Hume and Kant. We have already made some incidental references to Hume's theories. In the next chapter we shall consider in more detail, and more critically, his treatment of imagination. The following chapter will be concerned with Kant.

X

HUME'S TREATMENT OF IMAGINATION

Berkeley and Hume compared
'Imagination doth denote the mind active,' said Berkeley. And the activity of the mind, finite as well as infinite, was a cardinal point in his philosophy. Imagination showed that minds, or spirits, to use the term Berkeley preferred, were causal agents. When we imagine we ourselves produce the ideas we experience.

Important also for his philosophy is his division of ideas, a division which yields ideas of sense and ideas of imagination; sensible ideas are 'allowed to have more reality in them, that is, to be more strong, orderly and coherent than the creatures of the mind [i.e. ideas of imagination]'.[1]

Both these Berkeleian principles, first, imagination as a witness to the causality of minds, and, secondly the sense-imagination dichotomy, are considered in Hume's *Treatise*. Both, to speak roundly, are rejected. Imagination does not, Hume believes, prove the mind to be active: 'Nor,' he writes, 'is the empire of the will over our mind more intelligible.'[2] All we know is that we exert our will, e.g. decide to visualize the street outside, *and* the image comes. Sequence is observed, but nothing more.

Berkeley's second principle is also rejected by Hume, though the opposition is here less sharp. Where Berkeley has a two-fold division, Hume has a three-fold. Hume distinguishes between ideas of memory and ideas of imagination.[3] Berkeley has no such distinction, and indeed has little or nothing to

---

[1] *A Treatise concerning the Principles of Human Knowledge*, S. 33.
[2] *Treatise*, S. 632, E.I.159. See also his *Enquiry concerning Human Understanding*, 53.
[3] *Treatise*, I. 1.3.

say about memory in any of his writings. Presumably his position would be that remembering is one operation in which ideas of imagination are concerned, imagining is another. Hume prefers to make the distinction, not in terms of mental operations, but of objects. Ideas of memory retain a considerable degree of their first vivacity; ideas of imagination have entirely lost their vivacity and become 'perfect' ideas.

Though, as we have seen, imagination is an important matter for Berkeley's theory of spirits and their agency, he is content to make that point and to pass on to other topics. Hume, on the contrary, is constantly referring to imagination. Whereas an intellectualist philosopher will solve problems by recourse to reason or intellect, Hume's universal remedy is imagination. Imagination for him plays a key part in our perception of the external world. Imagination is allied to sympathy, the linchpin of Hume's moral theory.[1] This invoking of imagination to solve intellectual problems is indeed a strange procedure. We naturally ask, Why is imagination so prominent in Hume's thought? And this question prompts another. What exactly did Hume mean by imagination? There are critical and historical questions also to be considered: What is true in Hume's theory? How far, if at all did he modify his views on the present subject?

Let us begin with the first of the questions we have just noted.

Why is imagination so prominent in Hume's philosophy?

There is a two-fold answer to this question. First, to think is, for Hume, to have ideas. But all ideas are for him images. Hence to think is to have images, i.e. to imagine. A theory of thinking will be a theory of imagining. We therefore find Hume using 'imagination' where another man, uncommitted to the view that all ideas are images, would employ 'thought' or 'mind'. Sometimes, of course, Hume forgets, and we find him using 'mind' in a context where his theory would require

[1] *Treatise*, S. 318f., E.II.42 f.

'imagination'; e.g. compare 'the *imagination*, when set into any train of thinking . . .' and 'as the *mind* is once in the train of observing an uniformity. . . .'[1]

But there is another, and more interesting, reason why imagination is prominent in Hume's writings. Not only did consistency, a dull thing, demand a star role for the faculty, there was also the fact that Hume did assign unprecedented functions to imagination. It was his opinion that certain of our beliefs—beliefs of the common man—cannot be accounted for completely by reference to present experience (impressions), past experience (memory) or reasoning. In a full description of how these beliefs are formed the imagination—and moreover, a remarkable property of the imagination—has, in Hume's opinion, a central place. In morals also imagination has a distinctive and crucial function: it is an important agent in the process by which sympathy is produced.[2]

These reasons why imagination is prominent in Hume's philosophy we shall study in more detail later. We may note here that the phrase 'prominent in Hume's philosophy' needs revision: 'prominent in Hume's *Treatise*' is more accurate, for the faculty is much less evident in the *Enquiries*. And the question arises, Have we here a change of view, or what? Before we examine this matter, however, or pursue further our discussion of the reasons why Hume made such a liberal use of the term 'imagination', we must first consider another of the problems we listed above, namely, What exactly did Hume mean by the term?

What did Hume mean by 'imagination'?

The account that follows owes much to Professor Kemp Smith's discussion in his commentary on Hume's philosophy.[3] I shall, indeed, be parting company with him on one point of

---

[1] Italics mine, S. 198, E.I.192.
[2] S. 427, E.II.137.
[3] N. Kemp Smith, *The Philosophy of David Hume*, London, Macmillan, 1941, pp. 459-63.

importance. He considers that whereas Hume employs 'imagination' in two senses in the *Treatise,* one of these senses is rejected in the *Enquiry concerning Human Understanding.* I shall argue that the sense is not rejected, but merely omitted, and that the omission can be reasonably explained.

We may begin by probing into the two senses mentioned. Here we cannot do better than quote Kemp Smith:

'Imagination, as ordinarily understood, is the faculty which deals with those "perceptions" which allow of being distinguished from impressions, and which in proportion as they become "perfect ideas" . . . can be freely conjoined or separated. The "feigning" of which the imagination is thereby made capable sets it in contrast alike to sense-perception, to "judgment" and to memory. In the second, very special sense in which Hume has chosen to employ "imagination", it has an almost directly opposite meaning, namely as signifying "vivacity of conception", and therefore, in accordance with his early doctrine of belief, as being the title appropriate to those mental processes through which *realities* are apprehended, i.e. as signifying those very faculties with which imagination in its current sense has to be contrasted.'[1]

And he continues with a passage from the *Treatise* (p. 265), which ends with the well-known statement, 'The memory, senses, and understanding are, therefore, all of them founded on the imagination, or the vivacity of our ideas.'[2]

We have, then, imagination as the faculty of perfect ideas, the faculty of feigning; and we have imagination as the faculty which plays an important part in the formation of our beliefs—our perceptual beliefs, memory-beliefs and beliefs reached by understanding or reasoning. Moreover, and Hume grants this,[3] imagination as a belief-faculty operates not only in the case of such respectable beliefs as those of memory, sense and understanding, but also in the case of 'whimsies and prejudices'. The

[1] *Op. cit.,* p. 459.
[2] S. 265, E.I.250.
[3] S. 225, E.I.215.

distinction between the acceptable and the fanciful is given by that between principles 'permanent, irresistible and universal' and principles which are 'changeable, weak, and irregular'. 'The former principles', he tritely adds, 'are received by philosophy and the latter rejected'.

The passages quoted[1] are not, however, quite the whole story, so far as Hume's distinctions are concerned. In another place he makes a rather different distinction which for the sake of accuracy and completeness we must consider. The passage occurs on p. 117[2] where in a foot-note he explains that the 'word, imagination, is commonly used in two different senses; and . . . in the following reasoning' he had often been obliged to 'fall into the inaccuracy'. We might suppose that his two senses would be the same as those we have just been considering. But it is not too clear that this is so. We have, first, imagination as opposed to memory. Here imagination is the faculty of our fainter ideas, and this is in fact one of our first pair of senses. But Hume goes on to say, 'When I oppose it to reason, I mean the same faculty, excluding only our demonstrative and probable reasonings. When I oppose it to neither, 'tis indifferent whether it be taken in the larger or more limited sense, or at least the context will sufficiently explain the meaning'.

Light on what opposing imagination to reason means is given by an earlier sentence: 'In general we may observe, that as our assent to all probable reasonings is founded on the vivacity of ideas, it resembles many of those whimsies and prejudices, which are rejected under the opprobrious character of being the offspring of the imagination.'

The anti-reason sense will then apparently mean the faculty of whimsies and prejudices, i.e. those beliefs which 'are rejected by philosophy'. The two senses here are then, the faculty of fainter or perfect ideas, and the faculty of whimsies and prejudices. This latter faculty gives 'a more limited sense'. It is

[1] From S. 255, E.I.215, and S. 265, E.I.250.
[2] E.I.118.

the faculty of capricious belief. We may recall that in the other passage which we discussed Hume's distinction is between imagination as (1) a faculty of feigning, and (2) a faculty of belief in general, not merely of capricious belief.

It seems, therefore, that whether or no Hume meant his distinctions to be the same in the two passages pp. 117[1] and 265[2] he did not succeed in stating them as such. This inaccuracy, if we are right in so treating it, is however of minor importance compared with the question we must now consider. Whichever of Hume's passages we take we have a distinction between imagination as a faculty of feigning and imagination as a faculty of belief. Did Hume, we must ask, reject this second usage in his later writing, the *Enquiry concerning Human Understanding*?

The Treatise and Enquiry compared

Kemp Smith thinks that he did. He quotes in evidence the *Enquiry*, paras. 47-9. Thus Hume writes in para. 49, 'I say, then, that belief is nothing but a more vivid, lively, forcible, firm, steady conception of an object, than what the imagination alone is ever able to attain. . . . But as it is impossible that this faculty of imagination can ever, of itself, reach belief. . .' Here, it might seem, the view that imagination can be a faculty of belief has been, as Kemp Smith says, 'explicitly disavowed'. He sums up his discussion of Hume's theory of imagination as follows: 'Thus we seem justified in concluding that Hume's ascription of primacy to the imagination has no greater importance in the philosophy of the *Treatise* than that of being merely a corollary to his early doctrine of belief. On modifying that doctrine in the Appendix to the *Treatise* and in the *Enquiry concerning Human Understanding*, the reasons which had led him to extend the functions of the imagination beyond those ordinarily assigned to it ceased to hold.'[3] But now, let us look at the *Enquiry* passage quoted above. Does it amount to a disavowal? It is important to note

[1] E.I.118.   [2] E.I.250.   [3] *Op. cit.*, p. 463.

the phrases 'the imagination *alone*' and 'the imagination can never, *of itself*' (italics not in text). The question we must ask is, Did Hume say anything different in the *Treatise?* Did he say that the imagination could *by itself* reach belief? I shall try to show that apart from one careless passage, which he corrected in the Appendix to the *Treatise,* and which is out of line with his general position, he did not. Let us take, for instance, the passage which Kemp Smith has used as his opening quotation (p. 265[1]) and let us look in particular at the two sentences which immediately precede the quotation. 'Experience,' writes Hume, 'is a principle, which instructs me in the several conjunctions of objects for the past. Habit is another principle, which determines me to expect the same for the future; and both of them conspiring to operate upon the imagination, make me form certain ideas in a more intense and lively manner, than others, which are not attended with the same advantages.'

Hume is here clearly saying that the imagination, when operated on by certain principles, assists in the production of belief. He does not say that the imagination '*by itself*' can reach belief. The imagination is just one link in the chain. Nor, in the case of capricious belief, is imagination a sufficient cause. There are 'principles' at work here too, even though they are 'changeable, weak and irregular'.[2]

The only place I know of in the *Treatise* where Hume departs from this position is on p. 123[3] where he says that 'in the warmth of a poetical enthusiasm, a poet has a counterfeit belief. . . .' Here we have imagination leading to belief without extraneous aid. And this is what the *Enquiry* denies. But note '*counterfeit* belief', which half-corrects the error. And Hume suitably modified the passage in the Appendix. I think we may concede that the error was a gratuitous slip.

We may add that if Hume does not refer in the *Enquiry* to imagination as a factor in the production of belief, his account

[1] E.I.250.   [2] S. 225, E.I.215.   [3] E.I.125.

of how belief is formed is nevertheless substantially the same as in the *Treatise*. Compare *Enquiry,* para. 41, where we are told that association with an object of the senses or the memory gives rise to that 'steadier and stronger conception' which we call belief. This, Hume considers, is 'a general law, which takes place in all the operations of the mind'. If this passage had occurred in the *Treatise* he might have worded the last phrase 'all the operations of the imagination'. In any case, the theory of belief advanced is substantially that of the *Treatise*. What we have is the dropping of a word, not a change of theory.

I submit, then, that neither the *Enquiry* nor the Appendix to the *Treatise* disavows in any important particular Hume's views on imagination as expressed in the body of the *Treatise*. We have imagination in a wide sense as the faculty of perfect ideas, we also have it as a necessary link in the chain of events which ends in belief. Put in more acceptable terms, discarding Hume's 'faculties' and 'ideas', what his two senses, as described on p. 265[1] of the *Treatise,* come to is this. We can say that imagination is at work when we are building castles in the air. But we can also say that imagination is at work when, for one reason or another and in one context or another, what would otherwise be fancy is converted into belief; feigning turns into assent. In other words it is a fact that whereas we may be able to pass freely from say A to B or A to C, we are coerced to pass from X to Y rather than from X to Z. We have free imagination, which equals fancy, and we have restricted imagination, which leads to belief.

It must be granted that there appears little to be gained—indeed the reverse—by Hume's distinction, particularly, as we have seen, when we try to square it with the distinction he had made earlier on p. 117.[2] And we may feel duly grateful that only one sense, imagination as fancy, is retained in his *Enquiry*.

It might at this stage be objected, Well, if the omission of

---

[1] E.I.250.
[2] E.I.118.

imagination in the sense of a belief-producer is not to be explained as a change of theory, how do you explain it? I think the answer is to be found in the fact that the *Enquiry* is a more compressed work than the *Treatise*.[1] The former is a shorter writing and yet it contains more: its topics are more numerous. The compression is achieved by economy. And this, I think, is the main reason why Hume's second sense of imagination is discarded.

There is a revealing instance of this drive for economy in the *Enquiry,* paras. 124-5, a passage where the imagination is also concerned. Hume has been considering paradoxes relating to the infinite divisibility of space and time. He had solved these in the *Treatise* by referring to a tendency of the imagination to go beyond experience.[2] Thus, having noticed various cases of equality—what we might call carpenter's equality, engineer's equality, physicist's equality, we proceed to imagine a perfect—but he considers—fictitious and indeed false equality. This extrapolating tendency of the imagination he will later express as follows: 'The imagination, when set into any train of thinking is apt to continue, even when its object fails it, and like a galley put in motion by the oars, carries on its course without any new impulse'.[3] Our galley, we might say, leaves the daylight of experience and is carried on by its acquired momentum into the dark cave of fiction and illusion.

Now in the *Enquiry* Hume states the infinite-divisibility paradoxes and is almost prepared to leave them there unsolved as just another instance of the failure of reason. But candour wins the day, and in a footnote to para. 125 he hints at a solution, the conclusion of which is 'If this be admitted . . it follows that all the ideas of quantity, upon which mathematicians reason, are nothing but particular, and such as are suggested by the senses and imagination, and consequently, cannot be infinitely divisible. It is sufficient to have dropped this hint at present, without prosecuting it any further.' Hume

[1] I am referring to Book I only.
[2] S. 48, E.I.54.   [3] S. 198, E.I.192.

could very well have mentioned the *Treatise* galley-theory at this point. That he did not do so can hardly have been due to dissatisfaction with the view—it is quite a useful theory which he puts to good account in the *Treatise* when giving his ingenious explanation of the belief in 'body'. Rather, I suggest, we have here another instance of his pruning-knife at work. It may be added that the *Enquiry* contains nothing comparable to the *Treatise* discussion of the belief in 'body'. If it had, Hume would have had reason to mention the galley-theory; and if he had done so in that context he might possibly have done so in the footnote to para. 125, so that the two instances could mutually support each other.

So far we have been mainly concerned with what Hume meant, or tells us he meant, by imagination. We have, on the way, considered how far he modified his use of the term in his *Enquiry*.

Does Hume use 'imagination' in an uncommon sense?

One other point about Hume's usage we should consider. How far do his two main usages in his *Treatise* compare with the usages we have distinguished in previous chapters? In a foot-note already referred to, Hume implies that he has not used the term 'imagination' in anything but a common sense.[1] Is this in fact the case? There can be no doubt that his first usage—imagination as fancy, the faculty of mental images—is a common usage. It is the usage we discussed under the heading 'in imagination'. What are we to say of his second usage? Here we must consider separately the imagining of the vulgar and the imagining of the philosophers. When I, *qua* vulgar, imagine that there is now a wall behind me I am, according to Hume, believing something that is demonstratively false: I am accepting unperceived perceptions. My imagining can therefore be equated with supposal—false supposal. But consider now the case of the philosophers. When I, *qua* philosopher, imagine that there is at this moment, a wall

[1] S. 117, E.I.118.

behind me I am believing something that can neither be proved nor disproved. This philosophical imagining is not, then, equivalent to our plain supposal, for that supposal does not include belief, nor is it equivalent to our false supposal, because the philosophers' belief may, for all we know, be true. Nor can we equate this philosophical imagining with either our first or our third usage of imagination: the philosophers are not just day-dreaming and they can hardly be regarded as engaged in a creative, original activity. We must conclude then, and here we are on common ground with Kemp Smith, that Hume was wrong in thinking that his two senses of imagination were both common ones. The first is so, but the second is a hybrid: it is compounded of a common use, the imagining of the vulgar and an uncommon one, the imagining of the philosophers. It is this hybrid use, as we saw, that he does not employ in his *Enquiry*.

What is distinctive in Hume's treatment of imagination?

To what extent, we may now ask, have we yet found anything distinctive in Hume's treatment of imagination? His treatment, we may say broadly, includes a theory of association, of thinking and of belief. Let us look at each of these. The theory of thinking is the view that thoughts are images, i.e. pictures or copies of reality. And here we may consider whether Hume merits the title 'imagist' which has been applied to him and to Berkeley. An imagist is defined to be a person who holds that the basic symbols of thinking are images and that other symbols must be 'cashable' in terms of these. On this definition Berkeley is not an imagist for he allows thinking with the aid of sense-data, 'ideas of sense'. If we are to convict Hume of imagism we should need to know his view about thinking with words. Did he hold that words are cheques which must be cashable in terms of pictures? I do not think that he anywhere says so. Does he equate thinking with having or dealing with ideas, i.e. pictures? I think the answer is again, No. It is not clear then that Hume is explicitly committed to imagism.

Let us look now at Hume's theory of belief. To believe, he tells us, is to have an enlivened, vivacious, forcible idea, an idea accompanied by a special feeling. Hume has trouble in describing what he means by vivacity or by this special feeling and in the end he informs us that we all know what it is. If we look for the source of his trouble we find it mainly in his failure to recognize the dispositional nature of belief. To take a Humian type of example, let us compare recalling a visit to Paris with imagining a visit to that city. The former is accompanied by belief; the latter is not. In both cases there may be imagery, but in the case of recall there are likely to be also certain expectations and other dispositions; for example, we expect that if we questioned our travel agent he would confirm that he sold us a ticket and booked us a seat. To believe is, *inter alia* to have such preparednesses: we are prepared to feel surprised, relieved, satisfied, and so on. Hume, therefore, in seeking for an actual feeling was looking for the wrong thing; he should have been looking for a hypothetical or potential feeling.

Instead, then, of saying with Hume that ideas are vivified we ought rather to say that they are potentially vivified. How this takes place is, in Hume's view, largely a matter of association. Ideas become vivified through association with forcible perceptions, viz., those of sense and memory. Thus we may begin by merely fancying a visit to Paris; then we manage to link it with a remembered visit to Venice and the Paris experience now becomes a memory.

Contemporary psychology might amplify and re-word all this, but in broad terms what Hume asserts would not be disputed.

But association does not work only as a vivifier: it is also a factor in the ordering of ideas. Much has been written about association both before and after Hume, but there is one detail in his treatment which can be regarded as his special contri-

bution to the subject. This is his galley-theory. We have referred to it incidentally already, but we must now consider it
more closely. The theory, as we noted, appears in two contexts,
first in connection with the formation of such concepts as perfect equality, perfect identity of colour or a perfect octave, and
secondly as a stage in the process by which we come to believe
in 'body'.

To take the first context: experience gives us examples of
equality, varying from the pretty rough to the exact—the
tailor's tape to the electron-microscope. Strictly, in Hume's
view, our exact notion of equality is just the most refined case
that experience affords us. We have, however, some reason to
believe that there are 'insensible portions' of a line. Now if an
insensible portion were removed from one or two sensibly
equal lines, we might proceed to infer that the lines would
be no longer equal. But we should then, Hume considers, be
using a fictitious standard of equality. The mind has reached
this standard by proceeding with the 'action, even after the
reason has ceased, which first determined it to begin'.[1] He
accounts likewise for the way in which we reach an 'obscure
and implicit notion of a perfect and entire equality' in the
case of time, of sound, of colour-matching and of motion.

Before we comment let us look at the second of the two contexts in which the galley-theory appears, the discussion of our
belief in 'body'. I hear, let us suppose, a creak behind me.
Such a creak has in the past usually or often gone with seeing
my door. If habit were the only principle available then I
should expect to see my door. But I do not; I am looking the
other way. Still I do tend to suppose the door is there. The
explanation—or part of it—is that the imagination when once
on the trail of uniformity, keeps it up, even to the extent of
postulating unperceived perceptions.

What are we to say of this galley-process? Are we to agree
that it is a general tendency of the human mind—shared by

[1] S. 48, E.I.54.

all? Or might it characterize only some minds, in some situations?

First, it is pretty clear that Hume is not in fact, whatever he ought to have been doing, thinking of the galley-process as one of imagining in the sense of having images. 'An obscure and implicit notion of a perfect and entire equality' could hardly be a mental image. And we remember the scorn with which Hume treats a theory that deals in unperceived perceptions. If the view had been, *per contra,* that the gaps in sense-experience are filled by mental images, Hume's scorn would have been uncalled for. The imaginative gap-filling, whether extrapolation or interpolation, is, as we decided at an earlier stage in this chapter, a matter of supposition, illusory supposition or worse, in Hume's view. It is, moreover, a supposition of the 'vulgar', an illusory fiction.

Can we agree? A proper discussion of this question would, indeed, require a separate book. The theory of sense-perception and the nature of scientific method are concerned. Here only the most summary of answers can be given. What Hume is describing and deprecating is, in fact, science—or, at least, certain premisses of science. When a mathematician treats of equal lines, he is dealing with that equality which Hume has dismissed. Carpenters' or even physicists' equality is not the geometer's concern. He arrives at his exact equality by definition—however difficult and controversial the process may be. To ridicule this is to ridicule mathematics. And mathematics works.

Similarly, continuing bodies and processes are a postulate of physics. The physicist cannot prove that the same things happen in his test-tubes while he is away for lunch as would have happened if he had eaten sandwiches in the laboratory. But to deny that they do would entail a very complicated physics. Nobody seems keen to pay this price.

It follows, then, that if we are not to dispense with mathematics and natural science we must accept the imaginative processes Hume deprecates; or rather, we must accept what he regards to be the results of such processes, namely, perfect equality, unperceived bodies or events and the rest. But there is the further question, Do we reach our notions of equality and of unperceived existence in the way Hume describes? How valid is his account of imaginative interpolation and extrapolation as a description of how our minds work? Take equality. Do we reach it by letting our galley glide on into the dim cavern until we are halted by its inner wall? The implication, accepted by Hume, is that our notion of perfect equality is obscure, or worse. In fact, however, the mathematician proceeds differently. He observes a rough equality by using his senses; he is then prompted to make a definition. The definition will owe something to the experiences which prompted it, though possibly not very much. The mathematician who propounds it will certainly offer it as a clear conception, and would refuse to accept the dark-cavern allegory.

Still, Hume might reply, whatever about the mathematician, plain men think in the way I have described. But do they? I suppose the answer is that sometimes they do, sometimes they do not. Reflection on a series of more and more equal equalities may lead one man on, but another man not. Similarly with Hume's other examples: musicians may look for better and better sound-equalities, artists or manufacturers for more and more exact colour-matches.

How does the other type of imaginative invention stand— the belief in unperceived bodies? Have we here a general tendency of the human mind, as opposed to some specialized interests? Let us see what Hume says. 'Objects,' he tells us, 'have a certain coherence even as they appear to our senses; but this coherence is much greater and more uniform, if we suppose the objects to have a continued existence; and as the mind is once in the train of observing an uniformity among objects, it naturally continues till it renders the uniformity as complete as possible.' Much more, Hume adds, needs to be said to explain 'so vast an edifice, as is that of the continued existence of all external bodies'. And this he proceeds to say.

Why does Hume think we must invoke this tendency of the mind, what Professor Price has called Hume's 'inertia-principle'?[1] Hume thinks we must invoke this tendency because he believes that the supposition of unperceived objects cannot be explained by appeal to past experience only. His argument here[2] is not easy to follow, but it seems to hinge on the distinction between 'objects of sense' and 'mere perceptions'. Our 'mere perceptions' have shown in the past a certain degree of regularity. But in postulating unperceived *objects* we are exceeding what past experience would justify. Objects as perceived by us in the past are frequently interrupted. What we are now doing is to suppose an unperceived existence in order to save the hypothesis that our past experience has been of *uninterrupted* objects. The supposition therefore calls for some explanation, and part of this explanation comes from the inertia-principle.

Hume completes his explanation by studying the 'constancy' of our experience and noting how the supposition of continued existence is converted into belief. This treatment of constancy, however, takes us beyond the galley-theory which is concerned only with coherence.

Hume, of course, is far from sympathizing with the movement of the imagination he has described. The vulgar belief in unperceived perceptions, though explicable, is false. And he compares this belief with two other pieces of imaginative acceptance. There is the belief in causality, also grounded on imagination; this belief may or may not be true. And there is the philosopher's belief in a double existence—matter and sense-perceptions—which also may or may not be true: it can be contrary to the belief in causality.[3] Thus we have one case of imagination leading to a clearly false belief and two other cases in which we believe without reason.

Hume's galley-theory as an explanation, or part-explana-

[1] H. H. Price's *Hume's Theory of the External World*, Oxford, Clarendon Press, 1950, p. 55.
[2] S. 197, E.I.191.
[3] S. 266, E.I.251 f.

8

110

tion, of the belief in 'body' obviously raises a number of large questions. Is he right, for example, in thinking that the belief in question cannot be explained by past experience? Is the explanation he offers sufficient? Does it cohere with other principles in his philosophy? These and connected problems have been discussed by Humian and Kantian scholars, notably by Professor H. H. Price in his book on Hume. To attempt to consider them here would be only to scratch at the surface and I shall be content with having traced the path which leads to them. That path is one route in the complex itinerary which Hume's copious use of the term 'imagination' has required us to follow.

Let us, in concluding our treatment of Hume, consider the use he makes of imagination in connection with morals. A survey of the numerous contexts in which the term imagination occurs in Book II of the *Treatise* shows that what Hume usually has in view is the non-rational connections between our ideas. Compare, for example, his discussion of property. He notes that the owner of a field is regarded as the owner of the river which borders the field (presumably as far as midstream), provided the river is reasonably narrow. We do not however apply such a principle to the Rhine or the Danube. The difference in our judgment here is hardly based on reason. Again, if a piece of land became wrenched from one bank and joined to the opposite bank 'it becomes not his property, whose land it falls on, till it unite with the land, and till the trees or plants have spread their roots into both. Before that, the imagination doth not sufficiently join them'.[1] Sympathy again is another notable example of non-rational connection. From the sight of a child in pain, I have an idea of pain. I think what it would be like to have the pain myself, i.e. the idea of pain becomes associated with the impression of myself; but the impression of myself is a lively impression and, accordingly, the idea I have of the child's pain is vivified

[1] S. 511 n, E.II.214 n.

111

and changed into an impression, i.e. I sympathize with his pain. If the child is, in addition, my child, the association with the impression of myself will be still stronger, the resulting impression more forcible and the sympathy deeper.

If we turn to Hume's *Enquiry concerning the Principles of Morals* we find, indeed, little or nothing of all this. Reason is certainly still subordinate, but it is subordinate now to sentiment rather than to imagination. And he dissuades us from enquiring into the origin of moral sentiments, particularly the sentiment of benevolence. But this difference between the *Treatise* and the *Enquiry* may, once again, be pruning rather than retraction. He wants in the *Enquiry* to stress the 'original' nature of benevolence; it is convenient to omit his account of sympathy and he had to omit something.

Summary

The upshot of our discussion of Hume is then as follows. The term 'imagination' is prominent in Hume's *Treatise* for two reasons: (1) because he equated ideas and images, with a resultant equating of thought or mind with imagination, and (2) because he held that some of our most important beliefs are the result not of sense or reason but imagination. Our enquiry into what Hume meant by 'imagination' showed us that, broadly, he has two main uses of the term; he treats imagination as the equivalent of fancy, and he treats imagination as a belief-producer, or, rather, a factor in belief-production. Imagination, as fancy, is free; as a condition of belief it is restricted—restricted mainly by association, custom or habit. An idea of fancy is converted into an idea of belief by being rendered more vivacious. This vivifying we can call a work of imagination, but it is imagination controlled by association. Imagination alone could not produce belief. Hume has also, we noted, a distinction between imagination as fancy and imagination as producer of whimsies and prejudices—capricious beliefs. But again something—principles, admittedly 'changeable, weak and irregular'—must intervene to convert ideas into belief. At this point we considered, but gave reasons for rejecting, Professor Kemp Smith's assertion that Hume later retracted the broad distinction between imagination as fancy and imagination as belief-producer.

In Hume's treatment of imagination the distinctive points are, then, the view that every idea is an image, the view that belief is a matter of vivacity, and the 'galley-theory'. The galley-theory appears in two contexts, the accounting for (a) such ideas as 'perfect equality', and (b) our belief in 'body'. We rejected Hume's treatment of (a), including his strictures on 'perfect equality' and kindred notions. As to (b) we traced the complex and ingenious arguments Hume uses in this connection and noted the large questions which his treatment raises. In the next chapter, where we consider Kant's views on imagination, we shall meet some of these questions again.

XI

IMAGINATION IN KANT

The prominent place given to imagination in Hume's *Treatise* is a remarkable fact about that work. But the fact becomes intelligible when we recall that Hume was sceptical both as to sense and to reason. Now Kant also gives imagination much to do; but that he, the champion of knowledge against Hume, should do so is less easy to understand.

Kant's treatment of imagination contains some of the more difficult things in a difficult book. On this his commentators, sympathetic or not so sympathetic, are agreed. It is, we are told, an original theory, developed by its author not long before the *Critique* was written.[1] In particular, the theory probably owes little to Hume's treatment; for although Kant probably read extracts from the *Treatise* in German translations of Beattie and others, these extracts did not refer to imagination.

Yet some common ground with Hume has been remarked. And we may conveniently begin our study of Kant by noting where he and Hume agree and where diverge. To begin with, Kant, like Hume, uses the term, 'imagination' in the sense of 'fancy'.[2] Imagination is important for Kant's aesthetic theory; so also, indeed, for Hume, who defines beauty by reference to sympathy, which is a product of imagination. These are, however, usages which they might have shared with other eighteenth-century writers. A more important comparison enters with the topic of the external world. Our belief in 'body' is for Hume a product of imagination, and the belief, we saw, exists at a naive and at a sophisticated level. The 'vulgar'

---

[1] H. J. Paton, *Kant's Metaphysic of Experience*, London, Allen & Unwin, 1936, I. 365.
[2] *Prolegomena*, §35.

believe their perceptions can and do exist unperceived. The philosophers replace this uncritical opinion by their theory of an unperceived, persisting matter. The vulgar belief is a product of imagination because it cannot be credited to sense or to reason. The philosophical belief must likewise be credited to imagination, though the belief does require some reflection, some reasoning. And Hume, as we remember, has remarked that imagination is motivated here by the desire for coherence, a desire which outruns the requirements imposed by past experience.

For Kant also imagination largely accounts for our perception of the objects around us. But whereas Hume condemns this perception because of its imaginative origin, Kant takes the perception as a datum, and as something that justifies the theory which explains it. Admittedly Kant, like Hume, knows little or nothing about things as they are in themselves, so that his perceptual beliefs may be false or inapplicable to such realities. Hume can eliminate his absurd belief in 'body' by some hard thinking in his study or resume the belief again when he steps into the street; the Kantian perception of the world around us, however, is less pliable; indeed it is the only perception possible for us. We might say that whereas Hume's prejudices are like spectacles we can remove or replace at will, Kant's perception is more like the eyes with which we see.

The two philosophers differ also in the room they allow to the *a priori*. For Hume the prejudices in question are largely due to experience, though the 'galley-process' does represent a contribution by the mind. For Kant the apprehension may be indebted to experience for sensed and remembered data, but the fashioning of this material is dictated by the mind, which here follows principles much more numerous and complex than the simple requirements of 'constancy' and 'coherence' specified by Hume.

So much for comparison of the two philosophers: let us now

try to state Kant's theory in greater detail. An illustration here may help. On a cold winter's evening I see through a window, as I pass by, the leaping flames of a good fire. I think of its warmth, the crackle of the wood and hiss of the coal, but these, alas, I do not feel or hear. This thinking Kant calls reproductive imagination. This is for him the simplest, bed-rock kind of imagination. But my thinking does not stop there. I think of the bright appearance, the warmth, the crackle and the hiss as linked together. Why? For explanation I must go back to some past occasion on which I learnt about fires. Then I was aware of brightness by sight, of warmth by feeling, or crackling by hearing. A 'manifold', to use the Kantian term, was given to me. Now, according to Kant, if knowledge is to be possible, this manifold must be bound together, synthesized. Only thus does it become manageable—manageable by me. The general rules or principles for binding derive from this source, namely, from manageability by me, or any other human being, assuming that the human understanding is in general uniform.

The operation of binding Kant calls the transcendental synthesis or imagination. He calls it transcendental because it is a condition of, not a result of, experience. His reasons for attributing it to imagination are probably three-fold. (I say 'probably' because Kant does not give us his reasons explicitly.) First, the synthesis is an operation prior to understanding. Hence we cannot attribute it to understanding. Secondly, it is an operation, an activity, to be distinguished from the passivity of sense. We must, therefore, attribute it to a faculty lying between understanding and sense. Imagination is a reasonable candidate. Thirdly, it is a spontaneous activity. Now, spontaneity or freedom is, as we found in an earlier chapter, a mark of imagination. Thus we have here a positive reason for assigning the transcendental synthesis to imagination.

To distinguish this spontaneous faculty from the stereotyped 'reproductive imagination' noted above, Kant uses the term 'productive imagination' for the former. Its duties, we must now note, do not end with binding data into single manageable bundles. The bundles themselves must also be related. Having synthesized the fire I may go on to think of its smoke ascending the chimney and passing into the air outside, of that air extending many miles above the earth's surface, of the airless space beyond it. Or I may think of the fire being lit, perhaps an hour ago, when I was tidying my desk after the day's work. I am thinking here of the objects around me as connected by spatial relations above, beyond, beneath, to the right of, and also by temporal relations before, after, at the same time as. And I think of these as public relations, relations that you would concur in. You would agree that the lighting of the fire preceded the bright flames and that the smoke travelled up the chimney. Here also imagination is productive. It is producing the thought of a public space and time in which public objects are arranged.

Having shown the reason why Kant chose to use the term 'transcendental synthesis of imagination' and explained how imagination, sense and understanding form a trio, we must now add that he himself may seem to have somewhat spoilt our tidy distinctions by speaking of imagination as the 'first working of understanding upon sensibility'. I think however that we may treat this statement as rather an indication that he does not intend to regard understanding, imagination and the rest as faculties, sovereign mental powers. We need not suppose him to be denying that there is a binding operation, which is both a condition of experience and independent of experience.

We may now consider Kant's theory of schemata, a theory into which imagination enters, though how exactly it does so is not easy to determine. The schemata are apparently rules, or the products of rules—Kantian experts differ—for applying concepts to the raw material of knowledge. When these concepts are *a priori* concepts, the categories, we have the

117

'transcendental schemata'. Assuming that the latter are to be interpreted as rules, then we have a situation which might be illustrated as follows. A man wishes to withdraw money from his bank. To do so he must make an order of some sort. The accepted convention is that the order must take the concrete form of a cheque (or draft). Now when he wishes to write a cheque, in order to withdraw say £10 from the bank, he must conform to the specific pattern imposed by the instructions on the cheque: he must write 'ten pounds' here, sign there, put the date in the corner. Having done all this, and presented his cheque, the £10 will normally be forthcoming.

Now the original order here—'an order of some sort'— corresponds to the category. The blank cheque is the schema. The filling up of the cheque is the productive imagination acting according to rules supplied by the understanding. The receiving of the money is the acquiring of knowledge.

If our illustration of Kant's theory is sound then the main point of interest to the topic of imagination that emerges from the theory is this. If the transcendental activity of the imagination is to result in knowledge then that activity must obey rules of the understanding. How far Kant has made here a valid contribution to the theory of knowledge is a point on which Kantian commentators have much to say. Instead of attempting to add to their opinions let us consider rather how the Kantian usages of 'imagination' we have distinguished compare with the distinctions we made in earlier chapters, between 'in imagination', supposal plain, false supposal and 'with imagination'.

Kant's productive imagination, though it implies novelty, a going beyond the given, has not the freedom implied by 'with imagination', for the synthesis the productive imagination makes must conform to rules of the understanding. Nor is the implication of being imaginary—'in imagination'— intended. The product is real, empirically at least. Nor is the result a false supposition. Can the process then be regarded

118

as supposal plain? That is, do we just suppose that, for example, a sight, a sound and a feel are linked? Whether the supposition is true, whether there is some noumenal basis for a connection between the three data we do not know; but we find that on this supposition, and on similar ones, we can make sense of our experience. To interpret Kant's productive imagination in this way seems reasonable. We may therefore consider the activity as an example of our supposal plain.

Kant's reproductive imagination can be classified more readily. Given lavender scent we think of lavender colour, even though the colour is not sensuously present: our eyes are closed, or it may be too dark to see. The colour is present 'in imagination'. This imagination, in Kant's view, is governed by association, by what has happened; unlike productive imagination, it is the result of, not a condition of, experience.

We remarked above that the productive imagination must conform to rules of the understanding, and that it therefore lacks the freedom implied by our phrase 'with imagination'. This remark applies primarily to the productive imagination when concerned in the acquiring of knowledge. When we turn to Kant's aesthetic theory where the productive imagination is concerned in judgments of beauty we still find that there is a conformity to rule, but it is now 'conformity to law, without a law'.[1] The productive imagination, operating with such disciplined freedom, does approach to the activity we described by the phrase 'with imagination'. And this is what we might expect; for as we saw in our discussion of art, we must use our imagination, i.e. act with imagination, if we are to make an intelligent appraisal of an artist's work.

[1] Kant, *Critique of Aesthetic Judgment*, §22.

SUMMARY

1. The term 'imagination' has three main usages indicated by the phrase 'in imagination', the term 'supposal' and the phrase 'with imagination'.

2. We may distinguish between 'plain' supposal and false supposal.

3. We may characterize the concept 'in imagination' by reference to the 'dimensions' of receptive state, content, belief, feeling and controllability.

4. Dreams are instances of supposal—usually false supposal. An alternative account is the 'story theory of dreams' which may be held in either a logical form or a factual form. The theory can be accepted—at a price; but the price may well seem too great.

5. The problem raised by Descartes of finding a 'certain mark' to distinguish dreaming from waking life is not a bogus question. This can be shown by generalizing a problem put to Locke by William Molyneux. By generalizing a question raised by Hume we can provide an answer to Descartes' dream problem.

6. The propriety of using the term 'image' may be defended by reference to the experience of the blind.

Differences between after-images, imagination-images, dream-images and hallucination-images are remarked (Chapter VII).

7. Three questions concerning the usage 'with imagination' are considered in Chapter VIII, namely, What are the activities that can be performed 'with imagination'? What are the properties implied by the phrase 'with imagination'? What causes something to be done 'with imagination'?

8. The nature of a work of art, how we apprehend such a work, its relation to feeling and to imagination are discussed in Chapter IX. We may need to use our imagination, i.e. to re-act 'with imagination', when confronted with a work of art, but it does not follow that a work of art is an imaginary object.

9. The reasons why the term 'imagination' is prominent in Hume's *Treatise* and the distinctive features of his treatment are discussed in Chapter X and summarized on pp. 112-3.

10. Kant's distinction between reproductive and productive imagination and his theory of schemata can be expressed in terms of the usages of 'imagination' observed in the present essay.

LIST OF REFERENCES

Recent published work in English on the philosophy of imagination is to be found mainly in articles and in books not concerned solely with the subject. The following list, which contains the publications most frequently consulted in writing the present essay, may therefore be useful.

GENERAL

Berkeley, *A Treatise concerning the Principles of Human Knowledge*
Flew, Annis, 'Images, supposing and imagining', *Philosophy,* July 1953
Hume, *A Treatise upon Human Nature*
Hume, *An Enquiry concerning Human Understanding, An Enquiry concerning the Principles of Morals*
Humphrey, G., *Thinking* (1951)
Kant, *Critique of Pure Reason*
Ryle, G., *The Concept of Mind*
Sartre, J.-P., *The Psychology of Imagination* (1950)

ART AND IMAGINATION

Coleridge, S. T., *Biographia Literaria*
Collingwood, R. G., *The Principles of Art* (1938)
Elton, W. (ed.), *Aesthetics and Language* (1954)
House, H., *Coleridge* (1953)
Kant, *Critique of Aesthetic Judgment*
Langer, S., *Feeling and Form* (1953)
Langer, S., *Problems of Art* (1957)
Macdonald, M., 'Art and imagination', *Proceedings of the Aristotelian Society,* Vol. LIII (1953)
Watson, G. G., 'Contributions to a dictionary of critical terms: imagination and fancy', *Essays in Criticism III,* 2 (1953)

DREAMS AND IMAGINATION

Baker, M. J., 'Sleeping and waking', *Mind,* October 1954
Descartes, *Metaphysical Meditations*
Kalish, D., *see* Yost below
von Leyden, W., 'Sleeping and waking', *Mind,* April 1956
Macdonald M., 'Sleeping and waking', *Mind,* April 1953

Malcolm, N., *Dreaming* (1959)

Thomas, L. E. and Manser, A. R., *Proceedings of the Aristotelian Society*, Supplementary Volume XXX, symposium entitled 'Dreams' (1956)

Yost, R. M., Jr, 'Professor Malcolm on dreaming and scepticism', *Philosophical Quarterly*, April and July, 1959

Yost, R. M., Jr and Kalish, D., 'Miss Macdonald on sleeping and waking', *Philosophical Quarterly*, April 1955

The articles by R. M. Yost above contain numerous further references.

INDEX

GEORGE ALLEN & UNWIN LTD
London: 40 Museum Street, W.C.1

Auckland: 24 Wyndham Street
Sydney, N.S.W.: Bradbury House, 55 York Street
Cape Town: 109 Long Street
Bombay: 15 Graham Road, Ballard Estate, Bombay 1
Calcutta: 17 Chittaranjan Avenue, Calcutta 13
New Delhi: 13-14 Ajmeri Gate Extension, New Dehli 1
Karachi: Karachi Chambers, McLeod Road
Mexico: Villalongin 32-10, Piso, Mexico 5, D.F.
Toronto: 91 Wellington Street West
Sao Paulo: Avenida 9 de Julho 1138-Ap. 51
Buenos Aires: Escritorio 454-459, Florida 165
Singapore: 36c Princep Street, Singapore 7
Hong Kong: 1/12 Mirador Mansions, Kowloon

OUR EXPERIENCE OF GOD

H. D. Lewis

How do we know that religious assertions are true? There can hardly be a question of greater importance than this for religious studies. It is the question with which this book is mainly concerned; and in dealing with it, on the basis of his account of certain religious experiences and the patterns these form in history, the author also discusses other topics of much current interest such as the place of imagination in art and religion, the preternatural and religion, the credibility of miracles and the status of dogma. The book has been written in the belief that religious claims become much more compelling and relevant to our situation today when viewed in the light of a philosophical understanding of their nature—an understanding which the author thinks has been deepened for us by recent controversies, and especially by the alleged challenge of contemporary empiricism to religion. The book has been designed to interest the layman as well as the professional philosopher and theologian.

30*s. net*

THE THEOLOGICAL FRONTIER OF ETHICS

W. G. MacLagan, Ph.D.

Does morality depend on religion? With this familiar question in mind the present work criticizes afresh the old, but by no means superannuated, doctrines of man's natural sinfulness, of God as author of the 'moral law', or moral achievement as the work of grace, and of the claim of love to be preferred to dutifulness. Throughout, the self-sufficiency of what religious writers are apt to call 'mere morality' is upheld. Theological interpretations of duty and of our ability to respond to it are not only unnecessary but even indefensible, except in so far as they operate with the concept of non-personal Deity. How that concept can be combined with the personal concept characteristic of theism remains problematic.

In a brief concluding chapter, the author indicates how those who take both morality and religion seriously might best answer the question with which the book began.

28*s. net*

THE MUIRHEAD LIBRARY OF PHILOSOPHY

REASON AND GOODNESS
Brand Blanshard

In these Gifford Lectures, delivered at St. Andrews, Professor
Blanshard surveys a battlefield, the field of recent ethics. The
views of Moore and Ross, of the emotivists and the liguistic
philosophers, of Westermarck, Dewey and Perry, are critically
examined. From this examination there springs a fresh account
of what the central terms of morals mean — terms such as 'good',
'right', and 'ought'. The present debates about them, which are
often thought to be merely verbal, Professor Blanshard shows to
be the results of centuries of slow refinement of the issues. Indeed some of the most acute of ethical conflicts are rooted in a
tension between reason and feeling, between Greek and Chris-
tian ways of thought, and that are some two thousand years old.
This book attempts to state the issues clearly, to trace their history, and to make proposals for their solution.

42s. net

THE RELEVANCE OF WHITEHEAD
Editor, Ivor Leclerc, Ph.D.

This collection of essays marks the centenary of the birth of
Alfred North Whitehead. The continuing influence and signifi-
cance of Whitehead's thought is exemplified in the way in
which the various writers, who do not constitute a particular
school, approach their chosen topic of enquiry. While a few
devote themselves specifically to the assessment or criticism of
aspects of Whitehead's work, others develop Whiteheadian
themes and suggestions and still others follow their own lines of
thought to which Whitehead has been relevant.

In acknowledgement of the importance of Whitehead's
achievement for the contemporary philosophical scene, and of
the contributors' indebtedness to Whitehead, this volume is
entitled *The Relevance of Whitehead*.

42s. net

GEORGE ALLEN & UNWIN LTD